ABOUT THE AUTHOR

Nick Hall, Ph.D. is a medical scientist and professional speaker, who for over 30 years has conducted groundbreaking studies linking the mind and body. This research has been published in over 150 periodicals and featured by the national and international media, including CBS' *60 Minutes*, the BBC's *Nova* series, and the Emmy Award-winning program *Healing and the Mind*, aired by PBS. He also has been the recipient of two prestigious Research Scientist Development Awards, which the National Institutes of Health grants only to the top scientists in the United States. Nick is no stranger, as well, to the more pragmatic aspects of dealing with change and with making difficult choices. After earning his way through college wrestling alligators and milking rattlesnakes, he worked as an intelligence-operative for the U.S. Government. He also led a *National Geographic*-sponsored expedition to the West Indies, where he studied mass-stranding behavior in whales. While working in the islands, he endured the Marxist revolution in Grenada and the La Soufriere volcano eruption in St. Vincent. His practical insights for coping with change and adversity have been shaped over a span of nearly four decades. For example, in 1968, he became the first person to complete the grueling Baja 1,000 mile off-road race on a bicycle, while in 2006, he completed WaterTribe's Ultimate Florida Challenge in a kayak. This 1200 mile nautical race, which included a 40-mile portage, has been described by *Times of London* as, "the most dangerous small boat race in the world." At his Saddlebrook Resort headquarters in Florida, Dr. Hall presents highly successful workshops and motivational programs for some of America's leading corporations.

Visit **www.drnickhall.com** for information about his programs, books and audio series.

I KNOW WHAT TO DO, SO WHY DON'T I DO IT?

By Nick Hall, Ph.D.

Published by:
Health Dateline Press
707 West River Drive
Temple Terrace, FL 33617

First printing, May 2006.
Second printing with revisions, February 2009.

Nick Hall, Ph.D.
I know what to do, so why don't I do it?
ISBN 9 781424 304646

Cover Design by John C. McMillan.

ACKNOWLEDGMENTS

I've drawn from so many sources of information and personal experiences in putting this book together that I am at a loss to know where to begin in thanking all those who have contributed to this effort. The one exception is my loving wife, Hazel, whose contributions clearly outshine all others. Her patience and understanding while I was researching this topic kept me grounded and sane. This included keeping the home fires stoked while I was off on some adventure, testing the ideas discussed in this book. Also my two daughters, Rachele and Stephanie, each of whom has performed alligator wrestling shows with their dad at the Black Hills Reptile Gardens in South Dakota. They've also shared cross-country motorcycle and bicycle adventures with me, which is how I learned that the rules of dealing with stress change when loved ones are involved. I'm also indebted to the wisdom and example set by my mother, Eileen, who, for 93 years, behaved like a woman in her twenties, thereby, serving as an inspiration for all who encountered her. Finally, my stepfather, Max, whose hard work and dedication to his adopted family were unparalleled.

A large number of people have assisted with the preparation of the material used in writing this book. I'm especially indebted to Barbara Furtek, who expertly set about the task of correcting the numerous grammatical blunders and misspellings, which were scattered about draft copies of this effort. I'd also like to acknowledge her astute ability to spot statements with meanings other than the ones intended, along with the literary solutions. In addition, Betty LeDoux-Morris, a Certified Meeting Professional, has been instrumental in forging the corporate connections that have kept this book grounded in pragmatism.

Others have helped shape some of the described concepts. The conclusions of Dr. Irv Dardik, expressed in his Wavenergy Theory, have made me realize that stress is good for you and that it is only when stress is unabated by recovery that health will be impaired. Dr. Phil Hayden's research and insights into the ways elite FBI agents cope with stress under extreme circumstances have taught me that academic models have little relevance when you find yourself in a rapidly failing environment. I am particularly grateful for having had the opportunity to work with Dr. Jim Loehr, whose insights pertaining to stress and performance in athletes have demonstrated that there are viable strategies which can be employed to prevent stress from impacting performance. Some of the strategies involving exercise and acting are based upon those insights. I'm particularly grateful for the recommendations of Dr. Gerald Iwerks, a professional mediator, whose discussions on the subject of conflict have proved invaluable in formulating the strategies for coping with adversity. Finally, I am indebted to the professional insights of Geneele Crump, a highly skilled Licensed Clinical Social Worker, who also thought of the title. She has made valuable suggestions pertaining to the recommended behavioral-interventions and has assisted with the editing and layout of the book.

In addition to acknowledging those who gave direct input while I was writing this book, I wish to acknowledge those who indirectly provided assistance. Steve Isaac, founder of the organization WaterTribe, has provided me with the opportunity to test under extreme conditions while participating in WaterTribe-sponsored Challenges the recommendations I describe in these pages. Also, I wish to acknowledge my many friends at Nightingale-Conant, publishers of my audio programs, from which some of the material in this book has been drawn. Finally, I wish to acknowledge the National Institutes of Health, which, over a span of nearly four decades, has provided generous funding for my own mind-body research, as well as the research of others, which has been incorporated into the following chapters.

TABLE OF CONTENTS

INTRODUCTION AND OVERVIEW

I Know What To Do, So Why Don't I Do It? is about the most creative artist to have graced the planet. It's about a salesperson whose talents netted a fortune for his company. It describes a leader who inspired an entire nation and an athlete whose feats drew international acclaim. But you have never heard of any of them.

No one has. Their names are not forgotten; they were never known. They are the painters and writers and musicians who succumbed to doubt. They are the athletes whose dreams of winning waned with every loss. The leaders who never ventured forth for fear their ideas would be called impossible. The scientists who abandoned their pursuit of brilliant concepts in fear of professional ridicule.

Perhaps this book is about you, your child, a friend, or a colleague. Are you someone who eats copious amounts of fatty foods despite knowing of the link with disease? Smokes, despite an awareness of your increased risk for cancer and heart disease? Refuses to exercise? Risks injury by driving at excessive speeds without wearing a seatbelt?

And why don't you say what needs to be said? Or file your tax returns before the deadline? Register for that course at the local junior college? Finish that long-delayed project? Start the weight- management program you've been putting off?

Why don't you? Because it's not as simple as Nike's "Just Do It" marketing slogan. Sometimes, lack of motivation impedes progress. Yet, there's more than lack of motivation at the root of the problem. Many people have the will. They just don't have the energy. Too often, a compromised immune system is sapping their strength.

Then again, do you really want what you *think* you want? If so, is your lack of success due to reasons, or is it due to excuses? This book describes a way to answer these questions and provides an approach to achieving your goal, no matter what it is. It will show you how to control the things you can and how to accept the things you can't.

However, none of this will be possible unless you first climb out of the doldrums. No, not clinical depression, but the condition so many of us occasionally find ourselves in when we just don't bother. Instead of doing what we know we should, we busy ourselves with unimportant chores, creating the illusion that any action is progress. Or we blame fatigue and stress for lack of progress while failing to take steps to remedy the problem. It happens to everyone. Even elite athletes sometimes find themselves in a funk and unable to perform optimally when that once-in-a-lifetime opportunity presents itself. It happens to astronauts, surgeons, and law enforcement agents. Neither teachers nor nurses can escape the occasional absence of motivation. This book will describe the things you can do to accomplish your goals.

We all have within us the capacity to advance to the next level of health and performance. But, sometimes, the chemical changes triggered by stress and its emotions are so overpowering that you just can't do what you know you should. Yet, even though your life may seem to be in shambles, there are things you can do not only to survive, but also to advance to a new and even better state than you were in before.

'One size rarely fits all' is true in biology as well as in medicine. However, when you reach rock bottom, realize that we each suffer in a similar way. Furthermore, a similar strategy can be used, regardless of the unique circumstances that you may be experiencing. That strategy needs to begin at the headwaters of the stress response – the brain. Once you gain control over the

8

central command center of the stress-response, the rest is easy. This book will describe options for doing this.

In writing this book, I have drawn upon a large number of experiences, all of which have provided insights pertinent to the described themes. These include extreme adventure racing spanning more than four decades as well as formal training and research experience in Psychoneuroimmunology. Many of my core beliefs have been influenced by the writings of my great-great-grandfather, Charles Hadden Spurgeon, a noted theologian of the 19th century. He once preached to over 10,000 at a single service in London. His books are still timely and are hot sellers. At the age of 10, I left my native England to settle with my family in the USA, where I received most of my academic training. A long-standing interest in stress and emotions probably influenced my decision to select Experimental Psychology as my college major. I also spent two years training dolphins as part of an Office of Naval Research-sponsored study of stress-related communication patterns in dolphins before going to graduate school to train in Neuroendocrinology. My specialty was the study of the chemicals linking the brain with the body. Then I started over again at the post-doctoral level with a specialty in Tumor Immunology. When I eventually put all of this training together, my research interests ranged from assessing the effects of guided imagery and relaxation in cancer treatments to what happens when a stress-induced peptide arrives on the surface of a natural killer cell, thereby, impairing its ability to protect us from illness.

As a result of my broad-based training and eclectic research interests, I view the body in a manner that is not typically depicted in medical textbooks and in physiology books, which present separate chapters dealing with the immune, endocrine, cardiovascular systems, and so forth. Instead, I believe each of these systems should be considered as inextricably related to the others. So, perturbing one is going to have a profound impact on virtually all of them.

But, don't worry. This book won't be a stuffy, academic discourse. Although I was trained as a scientist – and, therefore, am a bit skeptical – I also have had a number of experiences that have resulted in my belief that the way things should work, based upon the results of well-controlled, laboratory studies, is seldom the way they really do work in the chaotic world in which we often find ourselves.

That's because of the rather unusual and very 'non-academic' experiences I've had. I worked my way through college wrestling alligators and milking rattlesnakes at the Black Hills Reptile Gardens in South Dakota. That was when I learned that it was wrong to believe I was invincible - courtesy of a 6-foot alligator that nearly ripped my hand off. I've also worked for the US Intelligence Community and have taught at the FBI Academy in Virginia. Yes, the rules sometimes change when your life is in danger. That's why this program will be grounded in science, but it will be guided by pragmatism. I now design team building events and present motivational programs at Saddlebrook Resort near Tampa, Florida, where I use this training and experience to help individuals and organizations achieve their personal and professional goals.

So, what have I learned about beliefs and about changing them? That there is no simple recipe for change…and there is no 'one size fits all' formula that I can neatly describe in this book. What works for you may have an entirely different result for somebody else. This is why I'll describe an approach called the Belief Challenge. You'll learn to determine what you need and whether the beliefs guiding your choices should be cherished or discarded. You'll learn practical skills, which have the potential to transform your life for the better, but only if you are willing to let them. That's because your beliefs are yours. No one makes you believe something. They simply provide the information that *you* use to create the belief. That's why you – and only you – can change a belief that might be keeping you from doing those things that you know you can, but you simply don't.

BECAUSE I'M TOO STRESSED OUT

There's hardly an aspect of anyone's life that is not directly or indirectly impacted by the global economic crisis. The stress it gives rise to has the ability to cast a shadow over your mind, body, and spirit. Genetics, lifestyle, medical conditions, the environment, coping style, and nutrition are some of the influences, which determine what your level of health will be. While it is true that not all people respond in the same way to adversity, once you reach your individual threshold, a series of events take place within your body which prevent you from engaging your natural healing systems. It's a barrier comprised of stress-related chemicals, emotions, and redirection of energy resources to elements of the fight/flight response. But this barrier is not permanent. It can be penetrated. Each of us has the internal ability to not just survive but to move onto the next, higher level of functioning.

Coping With Fear

I know what to do, so why don't I do it? Invariably, fear is a part of the answer. Whatever it is you know you ought to do or want to do is going to result in change. It may be a change in your appearance if weight loss is your goal. Or, perhaps, increased wealth if going for the promotion is your objective. Some people fear failure. Therefore, by not trying, you avoid the letdown. Others fear success. *"I don't deserve it"* or *"My friends will resent me."*

Whatever your source of fear, it will prevent you from moving forward. That's because the emotion of fear triggers inactivity. Better safe than sorry is a prevalent attitude that will keep you in that familiar rut, despite promising opportunities. At other times, you may be overwhelmed. No single problem alone is preventing you from moving forward. Instead, it's all those little things, which keep piling up in your life. You become trapped in a vicious circle, unable to escape from a downward spiral. That's when you need to clear the fog so that you can more clearly see the solution. Here are some things you can do which may help:

Reduce your consumption of saturated fats, including red meat and dairy products. The same deposits that can interfere with blood flow to the heart also can interfere with blood flow to the brain. Healthy arteries will help keep the brain in optimal working order.

Eat plenty of vegetables because the flavonoids and carotenoids protect against vascular disease, stroke, and damage triggered by free radicals. All of these conditions have been associated with illnesses characterized by dementia – including Alzheimer's disease.

Feed your brain appropriate fuels. Your brain depends upon all nutrients to function optimally, but it needs some things more than others. The B vitamin, choline, for example, is a precursor of a neurotransmitter called acetylcholine, which contributes to your ability to consolidate information into memory. Eggs are an excellent source of choline, as are soy, wheat germ, peanuts, and brewer's yeast.

Reduce your blood pressure. Hypertension is a risk factor for cerebrovascular disease. Elevated blood pressure may result not only in hardening of the arteries, but also in strokes. There is a correlation between elevated blood pressure and a decline in memory and attention. Exercise is helpful in keeping blood pressure at healthy levels, as is a diet of reduced fat, cholesterol, and sodium. Calcium is beneficial to maintaining normal blood pressure; so try to keep plenty of leafy greens and fish in your diet. Meditation

14

can also be helpful. Finally, treat the causes of snoring. If you sound like a wounded animal at night, it may be due to restricted airways. Treat the allergy or structural flaw; otherwise, the reduced oxygen intake can lead to high blood pressure and other vascular problems. You'll also awaken feeling tired, due to reduced oxygen intake during the night. Your brain's memory center and your heart will thank you for doing these things .

Take steps to ward off depression. Conventional wisdom says that a decline in cognition results in depression. The opposite is probably true: depression causes cognitive decline. If you feel depression coming on, increase your B vitamins, especially B12. Eating foods rich in carbohydrates, with a small amount of protein, may trigger a rise in serotonin, which has been found to alleviate depression symptoms in some people. You should also seek medical advice to determine if you might need a pharmacologic intervention to treat a chemical imbalance.

Use your brain. Don't let it atrophy like an unused muscle. Keep it stimulated, and the functional connections between neurons will remain optimal. This can be especially helpful during aging. Continue to read; take an interest in current events; and share ideas with others. These activities are your intellectual treadmill for optimal cognition. And while I'm on the subject of the brain, let's take a few lessons from this ultimate 'change' machine. Whether you want to change or whether you want to motivate others to change, there are some simple lessons to be learned from the human mind. Here's what we know and what we can do:

• The brain is conservative and prefers the familiar. Connect the novel part of a new initiative to something familiar. Reframe so the new approach becomes a natural progression, rather than an abrupt change.

- The brain is curious and, therefore, wired to collect and to process information. Gather as much relevant information as you can. Delve into the scientific explanation, which justifies the change you are about to make. Fear is the emotion of the future. It arises when you don't know what's going to happen next. Therefore, the more you know, the less you fear.

- In the wake of fear, the brain attempts to conserve energy, which is needed to fuel creativity. Take steps to reduce stress and the related emotions, such as fear, anger, and sadness. They will sap the energy you need to succeed. Stress also will trigger the fight/flight behaviors, which are designed to conserve energy for your survival, not your growth.

- The brain responds to images. You don't respond to the world. Instead, you respond to a visual or auditory image of the world. While you may not be able to change events, you can influence your perception of them. Examine your beliefs, which shape your images. Where did they come from? Are they justified? It may be your beliefs, not the world, which need changing.

- The brain seeks meaning. Whatever path you choose, make sure it gets you closer to your personal and/or professional goals. In this way, there will be a common thread linking all that you do to both the past and to the future. Your steps will become a logical progression from the familiar past as you make progress towards a healthier future.

Remember to take care of your brain. The payoff will be in multiple forms and for the rest of your life.

Responding to Adversity

At the same time the brain is signaling a need for more energy, it's also determining the best course of action. However, under extreme stress, the brain may guide you to do something based upon instinct rather than upon reason. That's when problems may arise. When you find yourself faced with adversity, there are three likely ways of responding. Each has a purpose; however, one creates a state during which you are more likely to take action without thinking things through. You feel the need to do something, even though it may be harmful to your health and well-being. It's called the fight/flight response and can be brought on by relentless stress. Each of the three ways of responding will be discussed.

The first and the most primitive way of responding is to do absolutely nothing. This is called withdrawal. I call it primitive, not because it is somehow inferior to other responses, but because it is the most basic way of responding. Low-functioning organisms - amoebas, for example, or other unicellular organisms - cannot fight or run away. All they can do is conserve energy and hope they will still be there after the crisis is over. In humans, this withdrawal response is directed by the vagus nerve, which includes the parasympathetic nervous system. This part of the nervous system inhibits digestion and lowers heart rate. It enables us to conserve energy.

When studying higher-functioning organisms – for example, reptiles - we encounter the second level of responding, or the capacity to engage in action. It's what Walter Cannon called the fight or flight response. However, this doesn't have to be to an extreme. Fighting does not have to be hauling off and slugging somebody. Fighting also can be standing your ground and not giving in. And flight need not be turning on your heels in a cowardly fashion and then running away. No. It might also be the ability to say, *"Hey, we've worked hard this week; let's knock off*

17

early and approach the problem again when we're fresh on Monday morning." Or, *"How about taking a 30-minute break and see if we can clear our heads a bit."* That's withdrawal, too. So you see, there are many different degrees of fight and flight. In humans, this action response, whether it is fight or flight, is handled, in large part, by the sympathetic branch of the autonomic nervous system. This is the branch that mobilizes us for action. It increases the heart and respiration rate. It makes sure that we have all the chemicals that we need to engage in the appropriate response.

As we progress along the phylogenetic scale to humans, we encounter a well-developed and highly convoluted neocortex - the outer mantle of brain tissue that encases the rest. The neocortex enables us to engage in higher processing, the third level of responding. It includes a branch of the vagus nerve that dampens the sympathetic nervous system. This keeps us from going off half-cocked as a reptile might, and it buys us time. It enables us to create images associated with what has happened in the past…compare them with images in the present…and then project into the future to formulate images associated with the different outcomes we are pondering. It is this sequential comparison of images from the past, present, and future that defines the process of thought.

Furthermore, this branch of the vagus nerve not only provides you access to your own brain; it allows you access to another person's brain. This is the branch of the nervous system that includes the neurons that control your larynx, enabling you to speak to others and to seek advice. For example, *"What did you do? What do you think I ought to do?"*

But these are merely words. They can convey information, but they don't do an effective job of conveying emotion. What establishes empathy is body language. It is very important while you are speaking with a person to move your eyebrows and to smile and frown appropriately. The next time you are having a conversation with someone you feel very drawn to - someone who really seems to understand you - observe them carefully, and chances are you'll find that they are matching their words with the appropriate body language.

The stress response can be defined as seeking safety. But what is it that we find safest? What is it we seek to surround ourselves with when we are under duress? We seek the familiar. The more familiar something is, the more likely we are to embrace it during times of stress. That's exactly why we gravitate toward our family, the people who are the most familiar to us. Parents have been there since the beginning. Or we might turn to a sibling or close friend. The body does the same thing. During stress, your biological systems turn to the most familiar way of responding. And the most familiar way of responding, the one that's been around the longest, is withdrawal. Next is action, followed by the new kid on the block, which is higher processing. The stress response includes progressing through each one of these levels, depending on how much stress you happen to be under. Here's an example of how this works.

Imagine you are dealing with a level one or level two conflict, which means the problem is the problem. Everyone agrees what the problem is. They may even agree as to how best to fix it. Plus, you have plenty of time to arrive at a solution. It is easy under these circumstances to engage in higher processing. Nothing has activated the sympathetic nervous system.

But now let's increase the pressure and take this to what mediators refer to as a level three conflict. There is now disagreement, and the original problem is not the only one with which you are confronted. For some people, winning may be more important than arriving at a solution. They may start to withhold information. They distort and embellish. They don't want to admit to anything that might be counter to their beliefs. Furthermore, if you make the wrong decision, there will be consequences. Oh, and, by the way, you've only got an hour to come up with a solution. It's at this point that a person is likely to drop from higher processing into action mode. Typically, they will throw up their hands and declare, "*Let's do something. We just can't go on like this. I'm not going to worry about whether it's the wrong decision. Let's just do something and worry about the consequences afterwards.*" That is a typical, behavioral *action response.*

Now the pressure is incredibly intense. There will be negative consequences, regardless of which choice you make. You have arrived at level 5. People are stabbing each other in the back, and you sense that no one is going to support you, no matter what decision you make. In addition to winning, some folks in the group actually want to destroy each other, cause others to lose their job, or to suffer personally. That is when you may very well drop into the withdrawal response and say, "*Look, I've had it. I'm not putting up with this anymore.*" This is a typical withdrawal response, accompanied with some elements of flight. Realize you rarely have a pure response in biology.

Clinically, withdrawal may be manifested as depression. A person withdraws from life, having little hope of enjoying pleasure. This can also be manifested as susceptibility to colds or the flu. After being bathed in the hormones that accompany an action response - cortisol and epinephrine, along with all the other chemicals that are mobilized - T and B Cells, natural killer cells, and a myriad of other cells in the immune system's arsenal--you are likely to go into withdrawal. It is after an episode of intense emotional strife that you probably will succumb to an infection.

Realize there is nothing wrong with any of these ways of responding. There's nothing wrong with shutting down and becoming reclusive when the circumstances call for it. You don't want to be out there interacting with other people, exposing yourself to pathogens, when your immune system

20

isn't up to the task of protecting you. That's when you need to be keeping to yourself and conserving energy stores so that they can be drawn upon to mobilize your immune system. And there may be times when you should not be making any decisions - when you should take a time out as you determine how best to proceed. For some people, depression may very well represent a turning point for the better. It may be the point when the person realizes, *"Hey, my beliefs and images of reality are not correct. I need to examine my beliefs and set about to create new images of the world."*

Of course, there will be a period of confusion during which it's probably best to do nothing. It's when you go into withdrawal or depression, and you can't get out of it that problems will arise – sometimes, requiring a chemical solution to get you back on track. And that, too, is okay.

And there is nothing wrong with taking action and not wasting time engaging in higher processing if your life is in imminent danger, and you need to take evasive action. It's going into action when you need to be spending additional time in higher processing to ponder other options that there will be negative consequences. Realize also that your personality or coping style may change as you progress from higher processing to withdrawal.

Under stress, it is not unusual for a person who is normally a controller to become an accommodator or the other way around. I learned this when by wife gave birth to our first child. I got caught in that transition period. Prior to that time, it was okay for men to just go off and do their thing. Hunt, drink beer, or play cards, and then wait for a letter to arrive in the mail informing them of the child's arrival. Things changed during the '70's. Men were expected to be there in the delivery room, which is good. It was wonderful to be there. I can vividly remember my wife going into labor - the contractions were getting closer and closer, and she was in a great deal of personal discomfort. She was unable to form words because of the pain. I knew what she wanted to say to me, though. I knew that had she been able to speak, she would have told me how much she adored me. She would have thanked me for being the means by which she was about to fulfill her dream of becoming a mother. Then, the Lamaze training paid off. The deep breathing exercises kicked in, and the discomfort subsided just enough so that she was able to express herself. She turned to me and looked at me with her loving eyes and said, "*Honey - you SOB!*"

I was going to explain to her that it was all right and how she had just dropped from higher processing into reptilian mode. And I was going to explain to her all about the polyvagal theory of emotions and tell her that she didn't really mean what she was saying. Then I decided, "*Nah, maybe I'd better just leave it alone.*"

I'm sure you've had a similar experience. You've been in a group and, all of a sudden, you've sat back and said, "*I don't believe that's Mary. The words she's using...the way she's behaving. I've never seen this side of her before.*" And she's saying the same thing about you. "*What on earth has Harry been smoking? I've never seen him behave like this.*" The fact is, neither of you has seen the other in their reptilian, or action, mode. And when people start acting in ways that are no longer familiar and which you can no longer predict, it becomes an additional source of conflict, making it even more difficult to resolve problems. You need to be aware that people do change, depending upon their internal, biological environment, just as they change, depending upon their surroundings.

Taming The Alligators In Your Life

When you find yourself plunging into alligator mode, and you know that you might do something that you'll later regret, you can bring yourself back. Begin by moving your head in the same way as if you were sitting in a rocking chair. Mothers soon figure this out. One of the easiest ways to calm an infant is to gently rock it. And it's learned without any knowledge of the sensory pathways linking the innermost regions of the ear with the parts of the brain that dampen the sympathetic nervous system. Perhaps this is why John F. Kennedy kept a rocking chair in the Oval Office of the White House. When his lower-back pain overwhelmed the ability of medications to do their job, he found solace through rocking. You might also take a deep breath. Expanding the chest muscles has a way of activating other parts of the nervous system, which also help to dampen an out-of-control action response.

Something else will become apparent as well. You'll realize it's wrong to believe you can't control your stress response. You may not be able to will a change in your autonomic nervous system, but by engaging in the appropriate behaviors, you can indirectly bring about that change.

It's time for a mental break.

Take a deep breath, and imagine you are at the Grand Canyon, standing on the north rim taking in the beautiful, panoramic vista. It's late in the day, the sun is beginning to set, and the sky is turning beautiful shades of red and orange. You hear the distant cry of birds, while a cool breeze brushes your cheek. And then, you slip. Your body picks up momentum as it begins to turn. Now, imagine reaching out and grabbing a tree branch a split second before plummeting into the canyon below. Make two fists, and hold on as hard as you can. Your life depends upon it. I want you to squeeze to the point that you actually feel uncomfortable. You must hold on for dear life...........

All right you can stop.

As you held on to that imaginary branch, did you close your eyes? Many people do when I conduct this exercise at workshops I present. Why would you do that? Oh, I can understand why you might not want to look down, but wouldn't it make sense to keep your eyes open so that you can see when help might approach? Or, to observe other resources you might use to extricate yourself from the emergency? Or, like others, did you hold your breath? Why on earth would you do that? If there were ever a time to sustain aerobic metabolism, it's when your life is hanging in the balance. That's when you need to get oxygen to the muscles.

If you could peer deep inside your brain, you would see in a little place called the *nucleus locus coeruleus* – and, yes, I agree that the person who came up with that name should be shot - a huge amount of electrical activity and the outpouring of copious amounts of norepinephrine. That brain chemical is increasing the signal to noise ratio. What this means is, it is focusing your attention on what the body considers important at the expense of things that aren't. If you held your breath, that was a way of conserving energy. Your body was preparing for withdrawal. That might have been fine at one point in our evolutionary history, but not anymore. It no longer has any survival value. Still, under stress, a lot of people revert to old, familiar behaviors that once might have been beneficial, but they no longer are.

During earthquakes, it is not uncommon for people to climb to the top of a tall building, in the same manner that their ancestor would have climbed a tree to escape a saber-toothed tiger. They see the ground opening up and decide that the best thing to do is put as much distance between themselves and the danger, so they go up. In fact, that's the worst thing they could do. It's a very unsafe place to be. And if they were able to engage the higher processing centers of their brain, instead of dropping into action mode, they would be down on the ground, away from any falling objects. But, sometimes, when we leave it up to the body to decide, it will revert to a way of responding that is most familiar.

24

Early in my career, I conducted a study delving into why whales swim onto beaches and strand themselves. While working on this *National Geographic*-sponsored study, I concluded that they are reverting to a very primitive behavior, which would have served them well when they used to live on land and, occasionally, ventured into the sea. When danger lurks in the form of predatory sharks, they might have escaped the danger by heading to the nearest beach. When they were in a transition stage of evolution similar to where sea lions are today, that would have been a good strategy. However, now it's extremely detrimental because they no longer have the cooling effect of the water to prevent hyperthermia. Once they've been beached for an extended period, they are doomed.

That's the kind of thing that can happen if you leave it strictly to the body. It will revert to a primitive belief that may no longer be beneficial. If you haven't prepared, you're taking a chance on which familiar way of responding is going to emerge. It's why you must create new and familiar ways of responding during times of crisis, so that you don't inappropriately drop into action or withdrawal when better options are available.

How can you do this? How on earth can you replace ancient ways of responding, dating all the way back to childhood, with a better and equally familiar plan? Very simply. Practice. What athletes refer to as training. What actors call rehearsing. If you saw the Bill Moyer's production on PBS called *Healing and the Mind*, you may be familiar with the research I'm going to tell you about. It's a study that I did with professional actors. I had them perform completely opposite roles. One was a very negative, depressed role. The other was a euphoric, upbeat role. Each play lasted approximately 30 minutes and was performed before different live audiences over a two-week period. Blood samples were drawn before and after every performance to measure the immune system and stress-linked, endocrine profiles of the actors. I also used computerized

25

heart rate monitors to assess sympathetic arousal, a physiological barometer of stress. Then the actors completed the Spielburger State Anxiety Scale to be sure their perception of stress matched their physiology. I also measured the same thing by using the audience, recognizing that how the audience responds to a performance will influence the actors. Briefly, what I found is that when the actor was portraying the negative, depressed role, the immune system went down. But, not when the actor portrayed the upbeat role. By creating a new image using a theatrical script, it is actually possible to change the cells of our internal, healing system.

Acting is something you can learn. Realize that I'm using the word *acting* as a means by which to elicit a true emotion. A lot of people, when they hear the word *acting*, think, *faking it*. *"Fake it till you make it,"* is a common expression. But that's not what I'm referring to. You don't have to be an Oscar-winning actor to be able to use this process as a means to replace old patterns of response with new ones. Think back to that one, glorious moment – hopefully, you've had more than one, glorious moment – but, think back to that moment when psychologists would say you were in the flow. Athletes would refer to being in the zone. Everything is clicking. It feels as though you could do whatever you are doing forever, non-stop, and never have to rest. You are loving every moment. Time is just flying. You've experienced that feeling. It might have been when your sports team won the divisional championship in high school. It might have been when you received that letter telling you that you had won an award. Recreate that moment. Refer to scrapbooks, talk to friends, and then recall how you were sitting or standing, what music was playing in the background, any aroma that was associated with it. Now create a screenplay based upon that experience, and start rehearsing. Just like actors do. Practice until it becomes a familiar and comfortable way of behaving.

Conditioned Moods

A few years ago, I became interested in learning how NASA decides who's going to get the keys to the space shuttle. How do they train a person to be able to handle this awesome responsibility and not become overwhelmed with fear? I had the opportunity to interview Hoot Gibson, the astronaut in charge of recruiting shuttle pilots for NASA. He showed me several, thick manuals. Each contained a standard operating procedure for every contingency that could occur in the space shuttle. The astronauts memorize the more serious ones. Training consists, in part, of being asked on a moment's notice, "*Smoke in the cockpit. What are you going to do?*" The person has to rattle off the protocol, and, of course, they sit in the simulator, pushing the right buttons and flipping the right switches. Not only do they create an explicit or conscious memory of what has to be done by mentally rehearsing it, they also create an implicit or subconscious memory of what has to be done. Implicit memory is what you do automatically without thinking about it. For example, the athlete who automatically moves her body in precisely the right way to score the winning point. Or the concert pianist who can carry on a conversation while the music automatically flows out of his fingers. Explicit memory is what you are consciously aware of. "*Where did I leave my keys?*" Or, "*I'm sorry; I can't remember your name.*" By developing an implicit memory, the astronauts are able to respond so quickly during an emergency that there is no time for an emotion to overwhelm them. They access a new, learned way of responding, instead of resorting to an ancient, perhaps outmoded, response. The practice also instills confidence that they are in control. Remember, it's when you lack control that problems are going to arise. I've used an example of performance. The fact is that you can use this technique for virtually anything. Are you a person who has a difficult time saying no? Then recall that occasion when you were assertive, and everything turned out just the way you wanted. And practice.

There's one more thing you need to do. Every time you practice putting yourself into that state of mind, link it to a conditioned stimulus, which will function as the equivalent of Pavlov's bell. It doesn't matter what that stimulus is: a photograph, a memento, or, perhaps, a selection of music connected with the occasion. Just choose something that will help put you in that state when you need to be there. A lot of people do this without even realizing it. You do it when you go on vacation, and you buy a souvenir. You stand there at the theme park and gleefully rip off one traveler's check after another for a cheap piece of junk that you could buy at Wal-Mart for a fraction of the price. But it won't mean the same thing because what you are really doing is buying a conditioned stimulus – something to help link you with that wonderful experience. Later, in the dead of winter when you're snowed in, you can now look at the object and be transported in mind and spirit to that wonderful vacation. We do it all the time. We are not simply buying souvenirs; we are buying conditioned stimuli that help us to counteract stress and create moments of happiness.

Do you know that you can tell if people are truly happy by simply walking into their home? You don't need to know them. You don't need to know anything about their health, their age, or their gender. All you need to do is spend 30 seconds in their home, and you can tell if they are happy. If what you see before you would give an interior decorator apoplexy, then that person is happy. Over in the corner is a chair that looks as though it has been salvaged from the dump. The spring is breaking through, while the leg appears to have been chewed by a wild animal. Next to it on a shelf, is a Statue of Liberty, a little plastic one with the arm broken off, held on with duct tape. And above it on the wall, is a picture that's absolutely horrible. The strokes of the brush and the colors match nothing in the room. But, if you were to ask the people who live there about those objects, they probably could tell you a warm and wonderful story about each and every one.

The chair that belonged to their grandparents and the wonderful memories that they experience as they recall having stories told to them as a child. The Statue of Liberty given to them by their spouse on their honeymoon at a time when all they could afford to give each other were cheap trinkets. The picture given to them by their child on the first day of school. I call it therapeutic clutter. Not filth, which is, obviously, very unhealthy. But surrounding yourself with things that are important to you without concern for what others may think. What a wonderful way to recover. If you have a huge amount of stress in your life, what better way to experience recovery than by walking into an environment where everything around you evokes these wonderful memories? By taking these steps, you will help to prevent your biological systems from taking over. You will be able to continue accessing those parts of your brain essential if you are to succeed in doing those things you know you should.

I've explained how beliefs and images you are consciously aware of can change you. Realize that your body can also be changed by beliefs and images of which you may not be aware. It works through the same principles that I've just been talking about —those based upon conditioning. I want you to imagine, for just a moment, a person sitting in an oncologist's office, awaiting radiation or chemotherapy. These are immunosuppressive treatments that are designed to destroy rapidly dividing cells, which, of course, is what a tumor is. Unfortunately, lymphocytes, the backbone of the immune system, are also rapidly dividing cells. So the trick is to give as much treatment as possible to destroy a maximum number of tumor cells, but not so much that you destroy all the immune system cells. The doctor wants to make sure that enough survive so that they can replenish and repopulate the various tissues.

Let's continue. The person is sitting there in the waiting room, flipping through outdated copies of *People Magazine*, looking at the obligatory fish tank over in the corner because psychologists tell us that fish are soothing, taking in photographs that are hanging on the wall. She receives the treatment, and her immune system goes down. She returns a few weeks later, but this time not for treatment, just to have a blood sample taken to make sure the immune system is rebounding. She looks at the same magazines, the same fish, the same pictures, and, lo and behold, her immune system goes down. What has happened is that those objects have acquired the same property as the bell in Pavlov's experiment. But, in this case, these objects are now inducing one of the side effects of the original treatment. It doesn't have to be those objects. It might be the entranceway to the hospital. It might be the song the person was listening to on the radio as she drove into the parking lot, or the taste of the Lifesaver that she was chewing on while awaiting the treatment. Ironically, it might even be the self-help tape she purchased -- the one designed to reduce her anxiety -- which now backfires because she listened to it too close to the treatment. By the way, what I've described is a well-controlled research study performed at the Memorial Sloan-Kettering Cancer Center in New York City, one of the foremost cancer research and treatment centers in the world.

This is a rather extreme example. There are others, although less well documented. You may not remember what you had for lunch on the day that you were in a car accident. You may not recall what song was on the radio when the telephone rang, and you received some devastating news about the loss of a loved one. But, thereafter, that same restaurant, that same food, that same song may very well induce the same anxiety-related, physiological response that occurred during the actual event. Your body makes an association between something in the environment and a response, but you are clueless. When you start to feel anxious, and you don't know what in the world is causing it, that alone can become a secondary source of anxiety.

This happened to me. In 1968, I rode my bicycle in the first running of the Baja 1000, a 1000-mile race across the Baja Desert in Mexico. I was on a bicycle, while everybody else was on a motorcycle or in a dune buggy. Consequently, I started a month before everyone else. Because I couldn't carry many supplies, I often would share water with coyotes and other wild animals. It was the nastiest, foulest stuff you can imagine, and I came down with every gastrointestinal symptom in the book. I was a walking microbiology laboratory, and I didn't get better until I had some good, chlorinated water, which I consumed in copious amounts when I crossed back into America. Do you know that to this day if I drive within two miles of a Mexican restaurant, I get ill? It has been decades since that initial conditioning occurred, and I know what's causing it; I understand the psychology behind it; I can even trace for you the brain mechanisms that are involved in this learning process. Nonetheless, I continue to have a difficult time shaking this biologically-based belief.

I have a friend who loves to fish. However, he's prone to seasickness. Whenever he went out on his boat, he made certain that he took medication with him. But he never read the directions. Instead of taking the medication before setting foot on the boat and allowing it time to have an effect, he waited until he experienced the initial signs of queasiness. Sure enough, the medication wasn't designed to work that way, and he would throw up. I realized what he was doing wrong, so I told him to be sure that he took the pills well in advance of setting out the next time that he went fishing. He followed my advice. But within 15 minutes of taking the medication, he threw up. .... *And he was still standing on the dock.* His body had learned to associate the medication with the symptoms of

31

seasickness. Sometimes, the conditioned response may date back many years.

This happened to a young woman who was happily married. Her husband was hard-working, a great father to their daughter, and a loving, caring partner to her. Everything was seemingly perfect in her life except for the stomachaches that would strike without warning. She went to her internist, who ordered up countless tests, only to find no evidence of anything wrong. He suggested that it was in her mind and that, perhaps, she should see a psychologist. This she did. The psychologist instructed her to keep a diary, detailing everything surrounding the onset of symptoms. Not just the bouts happening now, but also those in the past. She also was told to recall when they began. After considerable detective work, it was discovered that they started when she was four years old. Her mother had just given birth to twins, and from that moment on, her mother had considerably less time to spend with her. When she became ill, however, she did receive the extra attention for which she yearned.

As an adult, the stomachaches were associated with times when her husband was out of town on a business trip or when he was putting in long hours at the office. She saw the connection immediately. The stomachaches had become associated with getting attention. Sub-consciously, there was a belief encoded within her body that the pain of the stomachaches could lead to the pleasure of affection. Without knowing the cause of the problem, there was no solution. Perhaps a drug to reduce her anxiety. Or medications to lessen the pain once it began. But all they could do was mask the symptoms. The cause of the problem would still have been present, and she would have been exposing herself to powerful drugs with the ability to induce harmful side effects. In her case, just an awareness of the cause was enough to result in an effective solution. Once a tumor or other serious cause could be ruled out, her anxiety was relieved, and she was able to dislodge the biological belief, which stemmed from her childhood.

If you are experiencing aches and pains or mental anguish with no apparent cause, follow this protocol to determine if there is a conditioned cause. Keep a detailed diary. Do what the woman with the stomachaches did. Record everything you can think of, no matter how unrelated to the symptoms it might be. The time of day, the weather, what you ate, your level of stress, the songs you heard, even the thoughts that you had. Include it all, and then look for a pattern. You are looking for one thing that always is associated with what is troublesome. Yes, a conditioned stimulus can be de-conditioned, but only if you can identify what it is. Perhaps the answer to the question, *"I know what to do, so why don't I do it?"* is just below your conscious radar.

Cross-Stressing

Most people know how to experience success. That's not the problem. The problem is that very few of us know how to adequately recover from failure. As odd as it may sound, it is actually possible to train your body to do so. This is an important ability if you are to reach an elusive goal. There will be setbacks, and, so, having the capability to bounce back in order to continue along your chosen path is paramount if success is to be achieved.

I call it Cross-Stressing because of a principle from learning theory. When I worked for the Office of Naval Research during the 1960's, we used to go out into the Atlantic Ocean and catch bottlenose dolphins. We'd bring them back, put them into tanks, and train them to push an underwater paddle when they heard a certain sound. When they were first placed into the tank, the animals were clueless. They didn't know where they were or what they were supposed to be doing. The training was done in gradual stages. As the dolphin swam around the side of the tank, I'd reach out and gently touch it with the paddle, which I simply held in my hand. The moment the touch was applied, I'd toss a fish in its path. Eventually, the dolphin would make an association between touching the paddle and getting fed. After that, the paddle was attached to an underwater apparatus that the dolphin swam to on its own volition. This is called *successive approximation.* It's the same technique you'd use to train your dog. You gradually shape the behavior you want to observe and reward each successive step approaching the end-objective. As the animal started moving in toward the paddle, I would play a sound. Now it was only when the animal pressed the paddle after hearing the sound that it got fed. And then I'd change the frequency and the intensity of the sound so that, eventually, it was when the dolphin pressed the paddle in response to only a very specific sound that it would receive a reward. That was the ultimate objective: to teach the animals to discriminate between different auditory signals. It took them several days to learn this very simple task. But once the animal had acquired what was called a learning set, I could substitute other sounds or use visual cues, and the animal would acquire the new test in a fraction of the original time.

Every cell within the cardiovascular system, the respiratory system, and even the immune system has the ability to learn to recover from adversity. It is well documented that if the concentration of a chemical increases within the body, there will be a corresponding adjustment in the ability of the receptor to attract the chemical. It's one of the ways that the body adapts to change. By bathing the body's cells in stress hormones during their episodic release, the cells learn to recover; and, then, when a major stressor arises, these cells are better able to adapt.

Learned Recovery

The best way to learn how to recover is through exercise, yet very few people take advantage of this powerful tool. Some studies suggest that the average person spends two and a half hours a day watching television, yet only 15 minutes per day exercising. Many people get no exercise at all. Never in the course of history have people been more inactive, and never have we been more susceptible to so many diseases. Physical activity of any kind will help protect you against coronary arterial disease, colon cancer, breast cancer, and, without question, obesity and all of its health consequences.

Exercise is a form of stress. No, it's not in the same category as losing a job or a loved one because you are in control. Nonetheless, there are some shared features with your reaction to failure. It's enough that you can actually use exercise as a means by which to teach yourself to cope more effectively. The common features are:

- Increased heart rate
- Increased respiration rate
- A switch from anabolism to catabolism
- Decreased salivation
- Inhibition of digestion

How does Cross-Stress Training work? While each stressful experience and your response are unique, there are some features that occur in everyone. Thus, when your body learns to adapt to one form of stress, you are better able to cope with most other forms. It's like learning to drive a car. No two automobiles are exactly the same; yet, having learned to drive one model, you can readily apply your basic driving skills to all others. You may have to search for the light switch or hood-release button, but the essential components are about where you would expect them. The same applies to stress. Once you learn to respond to one form of stress or failure, you will have the basic skills to respond to most all other types. Moderate exercise is a form of beneficial stress, which can be used to train recovery. Here's how you do it.

There are many ways people exercise. One is called steady-state aerobics. Typically, a person will exercise for a set period of time at the same intensity. They might run 5 miles or work out on a bicycle for 30 minutes. That certainly is a wonderful form of exercise, especially from the standpoint of building endurance or of burning fat.

For optimizing recovery, it is far better to oscillate through the different levels. Each time heart rate is elevated, the body is learning to adjust to greater amounts of stress. Each episode of stress is then followed by a period of recovery. Plan on spending approximately 80 percent of your workout within the moderate stress zone. This corresponds to the aerobic zone and will improve your cardiovascular fitness. The remaining time should be spent oscillating between the low and high stress zones as you create a wave-like pattern of heart rate change. This will take you to a relaxed pace all the way to the anaerobic level, which leaves you breathless. By oscillating between strenuous exercise (stress) and a relaxed pace, you are incorporating a universal principle into your workout: *For every action, there must occur an equal and opposite reaction.* Or, for every episode of stress, there needs to occur an equal amount of recovery. Now, recovery becomes your familiar response following an episode of stress. Eventually, it will occur on autopilot, making recovery your default response, not just to the stress of exercise, but also to the stress of everyday hassles.

BECAUSE I DON'T BELIEVE I CAN

Without warning, a healthy, 28-year-old, Philippine-American woman was crippled with aching joints. Her face became inflamed and discolored, especially when she went into the sunlight. Her immune system was engaged in a form of friendly fire. Instead of attacking viruses and bacteria, it was targeting her cells. Diagnosed with an autoimmune disease called systemic lupus erythematosus, she was given drugs to suppress her runaway immune system. But they didn't work – in large part because she did not believe in either the treatment or in the powers of the Western-trained physicians.

When her doctor recommended a more aggressive course of treatment, using higher doses of the drug, she rejected that advice and returned to her native Philippines, where she sought the counsel of the local witch doctor. His treatment? He removed a curse that had been placed upon her. When she returned to the USA, the same physician who had made the original diagnosis evaluated her, and she was found to be free of all symptoms of lupus.

There are two things remarkable about this case report. First, it was neither published in *The National Inquirer* nor in any other sensational tabloid. Instead, it was reported in the conservative *Journal of the American Medical Association*. Second, neither the author of the paper, Dr. Richard Kirkpatrick, nor the editorial staff of the journal questioned whether the witch doctor succeeded, where the practitioner of Western medicine appeared to have failed. Rather, the question that was posed at the end of the article was simply this: *"By what mechanism had the witch doctor succeeded?"*

But did he really succeed in ridding her of her lupus? There are half a dozen forms of this type of disease, many having a strong, genetic predisposition. The ethnic healer did not

37

employ gene-splicing techniques to correct the mutation. The woman, undoubtedly, had a mild form of the disease, which had remained in remission for most of her life. It was only when belief in the power of a curse upset her biochemistry that the symptoms of lupus were able to appear. The witch doctor did not cure the woman of lupus; he cured her of her anxiety as only he could do in her culture. So, instead of being an example of the power of one type of healing tradition over another, this case serves as a wonderful example of the power that emotions, driven by a belief, can have in shifting the delicate balance between good health and disease.

Just as the woman's belief in the curse gave rise to the symptoms, her belief in the powers of the ethnic healer removed those symptoms. If a belief can alter the normal functioning of the healing system, imagine how powerful beliefs may be in improving other aspects of your life. Conversely, it's really your beliefs about circumstances that are preventing you from doing those things you have put off for so long. In this section of the book, I'll explain how your beliefs are blueprints - not for creating life, but for interpreting and finding meaning in life.

All of your life, you've been defining goals and setting objectives to get to where you want to go. But you never seem to arrive. Now, you're going to do something different. You're going to stop, look, and listen to those goals that you've been setting and see if they are connected to your deepest beliefs and values — and, if they are not connected, do you need to change your beliefs or your goals to create the necessary match? If you want to succeed in making positive changes in your life, you must connect your goals and objectives with your beliefs. The way you live your life must be consistent with what is near and dear to you.

What happens when your beliefs are not consistent with the way you are living? Your body finds some way to resist. It may take the form of impaired immunity. Perhaps you'll become forgetful. Or you develop high blood pressure. Any conflict between your beliefs and your lifestyle, if allowed to continue, will take a toll on your health.

Sometimes, you need to change your lifestyle - the place you are working, the environment in which you are living, or the relationship in which you're involved. Sometimes you need to change the belief – or at least take a closer look at the belief itself. Where did it come from? Is it really your belief or someone else's? Is it helping you to achieve your goals, or is it hindering your progress? If you follow the guidelines presented in this book, you will find the way to convert beliefs that are holding you back into ones that will propel you forward.

What Is a Belief?

Merriam-Webster defines *belief* as *"a state or habit of mind in which trust or confidence is placed in some person or thing."* Additionally, a belief is defined as *"a tenet or body of tenets held by a group."* A belief is an entity in its own right. It also shapes your perception of the truth. You'll soon realize that your beliefs impact every aspect of your life, from how your cells function to how you function in relationships.

The important thing is to know where any given belief came from and to understand how and why you internalized it – especially if it is a belief you want to change. You also need to recognize those beliefs you've been ignoring, along with those that have become habits and are preventing you from living the healthier, happier, enriched life you desire. Let's begin the process by identifying the 5 categories of beliefs. They are:

- Core beliefs
- Cultural beliefs
- Hand-me-down beliefs

39

- Advertised beliefs
- Biological beliefs

Core beliefs are your deepest convictions. Here's an example of how they can impact on life and death decisions. It's a comparison of how core beliefs affected the responses of two FBI agents I had an opportunity to meet while teaching at the FBI Academy in Quantico, Virginia.

One agent was on a drug stakeout, attempting to apprehend a dealer who was armed with a fully automatic machine gun. The agent, armed with his government-issued, semi-automatic pistol, had taken cover behind a wall. Bullets were flying overhead when, suddenly, the shooting stopped. Suspecting the gunman had temporarily run out of ammunition, the agent stood up, took aim, and squeezed the trigger. He killed the criminal at a distance of more than 50 yards with a bullet through the heart. The other agent was working on a joint task force with a local police jurisdiction. He was sitting at a desk near the door when a deranged gunman came bursting in and began shooting. The agent pulled out his pistol and fired back at a distance of just a few feet. He emptied the clip, but not one of the bullets hit its target. Instead, the agent was shot and almost died from his injuries. This agent, like all members of his profession, was an excellent marksman.

What was the difference? The agent involved in the drug bust had played football, baseball, and basketball throughout his schooling. Under stress, his body automatically reverted to a familiar way of responding, based upon a belief that it was important to win. He had an attitude that said, *"I'm not going to let that guy beat me. I'm going to win this contest,"* and that's exactly how he approached any challenging situation. Being under fire had the same, familiar feeling that he had experienced on the sports field during close games. He automatically went into a competitive stance under pressure.

The other agent had never participated in competitive sports. He lacked that competitive edge. He was also a religious man who may have felt that it was wrong to take another person's life. Although he would have been in full compliance with the Office of the Attorney General's deadly force policy had he killed the criminal, to do so would have been in violation of his personal *deadly force* policy.

Just as a belief had left the woman with lupus vulnerable to attack by her immune system, another type of belief left the law enforcement agent vulnerable to a criminal. I am not suggesting that there is anything wrong with the second agent's belief, or that a competitive approach to problems is always better. Problems arise when there is a mismatch between your belief-driven behavior and the environment in which you find yourself.

You need to know what your core beliefs are and avoid putting yourself in a position where your work or lifestyle may conflict with those beliefs. And you need to understand how deeply connected those beliefs are to your emotional brain, which, in turn, can impact your susceptibility to pain and illness.

Is your marriage heading towards the divorce court? Are you up to your neck in debt? Do you toss and turn at night unable to sleep? If your answer is yes, it's little wonder your life is in a rut. This inner turmoil is keeping you in withdrawal mode, which is keeping you from completing even small tasks. Moving forward may require jump-starting your system. It has to begin with the beliefs that are shaping your decisions.

Cultural beliefs are those beliefs with which you grew up. They influence your choices and value system. The lady with lupus was influenced by a cultural belief. It was her belief in the curse that brought her latent illness out of remission, and it was her belief in the cure that brought the symptoms under control.

41

You acquire cultural beliefs from family, neighbors, religious institutions, and just about any organization or person to whom you are exposed or with whom you identify. And they can work for you as well as against you. Cultural beliefs can be very strong and can run very deeply. Furthermore, the earlier you're exposed to such a belief, the more strongly it will be ingrained, and the more difficult it will be to get rid of. It may permanently shape your thought processes, rather like the wire restraints, which shape the branches of a bonsai tree.

Hand-me-down beliefs may come from any source, but most often they come to us from our parents or grandparents during our early childhood, at a time when we are most impressionable. They affect our career choices. Maybe you wanted to be a writer or an artist, but you always heard, *"You can't make a living painting or writing."* Relationships can be impacted, *"If you want it done right, do it yourself."* And even change, *"You can't teach an old dog new tricks."*

My entire life has been changed by a hand-me-down belief, which proved to be wrong. At the impressionable age of seven, I had arrived home from school devastated over having failed a very important math exam. The school that I attended in England was a carryover from the Dickens' era, and we used to get caned across the hand with a bamboo stick if we failed an exam or made mistakes on homework. It was a very strict school. There had already been the physical punishment, and now I had the belief that I was a failure. I was an emotional wreck.

My mother, a wonderful lady who I loved dearly, tried to console me by saying, *"Don't worry about it. No one in our family has ever done well in math."* And I thought, *"YES! I'm not really stupid. I just chose the wrong parents. It's those darned ancestors who gave me a defective genetic blueprint."* So from that point on, I never applied myself to math. I did just enough work to keep from getting caned, and that was about it. And if I barely passed the

42

course, I was happy as a clam that I got to go on to the next grade. I devoted all of my efforts to those classes that I did enjoy and that I did well in…then I went to graduate school, where I had to take statistics. Followed by advanced statistics, which is, of course, higher math. And I realized, with the help of a darn good instructor, that not only is math not all that difficult, but it's actually kind of fun, especially when I can see an application. And in my case, it was going to be a valuable tool that would enable me to pursue my professional objectives — a way to analyze the research data I would be collecting as a scientist. But, I often wondered how my life might have been different had it not been for that one, consoling statement from my mother. I might have become a CPA or an accountant. I might be working for the IRS, auditing your tax return and causing you stress, instead of talking to you about beliefs.

Advertised Beliefs. Let's take a look at what you hear repeatedly and how it affects your beliefs. Consider the word *stress*. It's used as a noun, a verb, and an adjective. And no matter how you use it, it usually has a negative connotation. I'm sure you've heard that 'stress is bad for you.' It's one of the most promoted myths in our culture, and it sells more books, magazines, and audio programs than even sex these days. The fact is that stress is good for you. It's a stimulus for physical, emotional, and spiritual growth. Problems arise when we fail to balance stress with recovery.

How about your immune system? Lots of advertised beliefs within the health industry promote the benefits of boosting your immune system with products…. echinacea, golden seal, garlic, tea tree oil, and green tea are just a few of the over-the-counter drugs people buy in an effort to 'boost' their immune system. Why do they do this? Because it is an *advertised belief* that boosting the immune system is the magical solution for all health problems. Well, that's a very risky belief. Do you know that too much immunity is what characterizes people with multiple sclerosis or rheumatoid arthritis? That too much immunity is the cause of severe allergies? This advertised belief has helped the health food industry become a multi-billion dollar a year business.

Biological Beliefs. You may not remember the salad you had for lunch right before that serious car accident. Or the country song playing on the radio when the phone rang, and you learned of the unexpected death of a loved one. But now, every time your body is exposed to those cues, you experience the same fear or sadness that occurred at the time of the event. Of course, sometimes the opposite can occur. A birthday, pizza restaurant, or photo may elicit memories of over-the-top ecstasy for someone you deeply love and care about. It's a conditioned response, which is a form of learning. You also can think of this as a biological belief. Without any conscious awareness, your body believes the same circumstances exist, and it responds accordingly. In a subtle way, feelings triggered by such beliefs could be keeping you from doing the things you should be doing by triggering withdrawal-inducing emotions.

I am sometimes asked to testify as an expert witness in legal cases involving post-traumatic stress disorder. I remember one case, in particular, because it was so disheartening. A beautiful, young woman had been brutally assaulted. It happened in a car, and, thereafter, that brand of automobile, that song playing on the radio, and even that fragrance which she had been wearing triggered a response so powerful that it set off the same immune system illness experienced by the Philippine-American woman who was plagued by a different type of curse. I'll tell you how you can change your beliefs in ways that will change your life for the better.

Beliefs That Hold You Back

"I know what to do, so why don't I do it?" Probably because you don't believe you can. Here are beliefs that I have heard as people explain why they do not engage in healthy pursuits. Many were passed on by clinical caseworkers, while others I've heard when presenting seminars to health professionals.

- I am too busy.
- I don't have the time to shop for the right foods.
- I work too many hours to be able to exercise.
- I have too many children at home to take care of.
- I can't keep track; I am too busy.
- I have too many family problems.
- Healthy eating is too expensive.
- I don't need to exercise; I walk all day at work.
- I have a low metabolism so I can't lose weight.
- I am under too much stress at work.
- My family cooks all the foods I like, and I can't refuse.
- I don't know what healthy choices are.
- I can't stick to a strict diet.
- I live in a dangerous neighborhood so I can't exercise.
- I lost the list of foods I need to stay away from.
- I don't like any of the foods that are good for me.
- With the holidays, it is impossible to stick to my routine.
- I'm not the one who buys the groceries.
- I have too many other health problems.
- It is too late. I'm too old.
- I have tried every kind of exercise and diet. Nothing works.
- I just take extra insulin if I eat too much.
- My doctor never tells me that I have to lose weight.
- My scales are broken.
- My exercise bike is broken.
- I am hungry all the time.
- I am bored, and I eat all day long.
- It's too painful to exercise.
- It's inconvenient.

- I don't have time.
- It's boring.
- It's hard to keep up.
- I'm too out of shape.

These listed reasons/excuses can be organized into 6 distinct categories:

- Lack of time (I'm too busy.)
- Lack of money (Eating healthy is too expensive.)
- Lack of knowledge (I don't know what healthy choices are.)
- Lack of ability (I have too much pain to exercise.)
- Lack of motivation (I know what to do. I just don't do it.)
- Lack of optimism (It is too late, and I'm too old to change.)

Upon further inspection, this list of 6 distinct types of excuses corresponds to the 3 major constituents of a person: Mind, Body, and Spirit.

Mind: Insufficient knowledge is a function of the mind. So is lack of time, of which you have plenty. The problem is how you prioritize what you do with what's available.

Body: Having a multitude of health problems can represent a formidable obstacle. While it doesn't cause disease, stress can create an environment within the body making it easier for the causes of disease to rear their ugly heads.

Spirit: Lacking the will to change can be an insurmountable obstacle if not dealt with. So is a feeling of pessimism. Chances are, the real obstacle is the belief holding you back.

Some of these explanations are legitimate. It's difficult to engage in healthy pursuits when you're struggling to make it one day at a time. However, others are merely excuses for doing nothing. The following Belief Challenge Process will help you determine into which category your beliefs fall.

Changing Unhealthy Beliefs

Whenever you encounter a belief - whether it's a core belief, a cultural belief, a hand-me-down belief, or an advertised belief - ask yourself, and then answer, these questions. I'm going to ask them in the context of how they affect your relationship with yourself, your family, your business associates, your neighbors, as well as the community-at-large. And dig deep for the answers. Plan to spend considerable time reflecting upon each. And don't assume that whatever first comes to mind is the only answer. Here they are:

- Are these your beliefs or those of someone else?
- Are your beliefs based upon experience?
- Can you think of times in your life when your belief was challenged by reality?
- Have your beliefs ever kept you from achieving a goal?
- Are certain themes reflected in your beliefs?
- Are you willing to change one or more of your beliefs if they are obstacles to your goals?
- Are your beliefs serving a useful purpose?

You don't have to wait. Begin the process right now by identifying a belief you would like to change. Pick one that is holding you back. Here's an example: *Better safe than sorry*. People are afraid of failure so they play it safe in both their personal and professional lives. You must overcome this belief if you are to be successful. Any change requires moving away from familiar territory. And any learning experience carries with it the risk of losing face. No wonder people stay where they are. Even though their business venture could have the potential of doubling its profits, or they might unleash the means to spend more time with their family by doing what they really want to do; instead, they remain in the same rut. We hold on to a belief because we have become set in our ways, and we resist change. We may want to do things differently, but we fear change. We are afraid of failing. So instead of taking steps to improve our lot, we keep things status quo. We even create new beliefs to justify the rut we're in.

I have a friend who services clients for a large company. His job requires that he log nearly 50,000 miles a year driving throughout the Eastern USA. Every hour that he is on the road, he is away from his family and those things that bring pleasure. He was recently offered a promotion that would keep him at company headquarters close to home. *"No way,"* he told me. *"I'm not going to become part of that rat-race. Too much backbiting at headquarters. I'd rather be on my own, even if it means a lower salary and eating in truck stops."*

Where does this belief come from? Perhaps from his early childhood. Many men are taught that they must be decisive and always make the right decision. Role models may have been present in the family or depicted on the television screen by our childhood heroes. Or perhaps through the pages of books read to us by parents. Subtle messages conveying what a hero can and should be were present throughout our early upbringing. What happens, though, when the child encounters failure and realizes that success is not guaranteed? Then the fear of failure may result in that person becoming indecisive or avoiding situations requiring that he or she take charge and accept responsibility. The person might seek employment in a subservient position so someone else can shoulder the responsibility for failure. Not only will this belief impact on the person's professional life, but they may also seek a spouse who plays a dominant role in their relationship.

While in some cases it might be necessary to consult with a therapist to help with the process, by asking the right questions, you can usually identify for yourself what is triggering a particular behavioral path. Often, just understanding the basic mechanism of what is going on and coming to grips with what the initiating event might be is all that it takes to initiate the first step toward change.

Perhaps your inability to express certain emotions is because of how or whether you were accepted by your family or social group as a child. Emotions often will be denied when they are seen as unacceptable to others. Consequently, you may repress an emotion through fear of rejection. A fear that originated decades ago when you weren't even old enough to remotely understand the process now shapes your decisions as an adult.

Healthy people are able to acknowledge appropriately expressed anger, envy, or sexual feelings without imposing punishment. People feel free to discuss not only their own emotions, but to be available as confidants for others who need to express their own. A person who has been raised in this type of open environment is more likely to take responsibility for their feelings and not to blame others for how they feel. As a consequence, they will be more comfortable with other people, and with making decisions, even if those decisions do not carry a warranty for success.

At Saddlebrook Resort, I teach corporate clients to accept the inevitable risks that always accompany success. These lessons are best taught in an environment where challenges can be created through realistic scenarios. Ours is a 5-acre facility, which includes a climbing wall, zip line, and other initiatives built high in the trees. The clients may be instructed to solve a complex task on the ground, or to get their team across a rope bridge they have to build across an expanse of water. Some activities may also involve actors to play the role of difficult clients or disgruntled employees. The participants learn to trust each other and to communicate under pressure. Our own research, as well as that of others, has revealed improved self and group efficacy immediately upon completion of the day's training. Furthermore, there is an increase in trust, and a decrease in stress. Corporations improve their bottom line, and, by having healthier and more productive team members, their shareholders welcome this type of investment. Because of demand, we now are signing up families and engaged couples, who use the program to enrich their relationships. Why? Because it works, it's fun, and it requires about the same time as a round of golf.

You can take steps to overcome obstructive beliefs in your life without going through our experiential-adventure training. Begin by asking the Belief Challenge questions. You are the only one who can answer these questions. Write them down, and then read the answers out loud. Sometimes, when you receive information via multiple sensory modalities, it's easier to process and to understand. Consider all the sources of beliefs that I have mentioned earlier. When asking if a given belief is justified, reflect upon previous occasions when that belief influenced your behavior. What was the outcome? Even if you weren't successful, was the outcome really all that bad? Bad enough to prompt you never again to attempt to move forward? And while you are at it, which decisions do you most regret? Those you made or those you didn't? Then list all of the ways your life may change if you accept the challenge of changing your belief and succeed? Remember, there is no single correct answer to any of these questions. But take the time to answer them. Collect as much information as possible. Perhaps the cost/benefit ratio will not be worth it. And that's okay. Or perhaps you should chance it. That's okay, too. You must decide on the basis of your beliefs and on the goals which they may impact.

Let's return to the notion that it is a mismatch between your belief and the environment, which leads to emotional upheaval. You always have two choices. When you have a mismatch, you have the choice of changing the environment to match your belief or changing your belief to match the environment. Some people have a tendency to do one or the other consistently. People who are centered tend to view the world the way it really is, instead of living in a dreamlike fantasy fueled by erroneous beliefs. People who are realistic about what they want know how to go about getting it. These people are open-minded individuals, who will gather as much information as possible, and then they are willing to adjust their beliefs if they realize those beliefs no longer have value.

In contrast are the close-minded people. These individuals try to limit the amount of information that they will listen to, and they will walk away from any discussion of a belief counter to their own. Such people are constantly trying to persuade others of the validity of their religious or political viewpoints, without acknowledging any other interpretation. These are the people who are invariably going to experience emotions that are negative and destructive.

But you always have an option. You can change your belief, or you can try to change the environment. Sometimes you have to change the environment. If you are being asked in the work place to do something that is dishonest or otherwise counter to your belief, it clearly is a good idea to change the environment and to get another job. Or perhaps your marriage has become so destructive to the well-being of you and your family that divorce is the only sensible option. That may be a very difficult decision. A bad relationship can be difficult to abandon because you may have a guilt-driven compulsion to keep returning to try to make it work. Such futile efforts may be driven by a belief that 'giving up is always bad.' Or they may result from an unwillingness to initiate change because, despite the turmoil, you are at least familiar with the status quo.

This happened to me several years ago at the university where I was working. My Mind-Body-based research program was regarded by my chairman as a bad fit for the Psychiatry Department I was in. I couldn't understand that belief. The program was well funded by federal grants, my students were winning national recognition, prestigious medical schools, such as Harvard, were implementing similar programs, and I recently had been promoted to the rank of Full Professor. The belief made no sense to me, just as, I'm sure, my persistence made no sense to him. I hung in there until the bitter end, trying in vain to change another person's belief to be consistent with my own. I felt leaving at the first sign of antagonism would constitute failure on my part - a form of *giving up*. *"There must be something I can do to change his mind,"* I kept thinking. It took a long time, but eventually I accepted the fact that you cannot control another person's beliefs or actions. You only can control your own. So I finally changed the environment and left. Afterwards, my only regret was not having made the change when the mismatch between my belief and the environment first surfaced. I still have no regrets because I learned from the experience, gaining insight about others and myself. All experience is positive if it fosters growth or new insights.

Of course, there are times when your beliefs are simply not correct. You don't have enough information, or you are focusing on the wrong type of information, in which case it probably is better to change your image of reality. And, there are situations where it isn't exclusively a problem of environment or of beliefs. You may not be able to leave a job in its entirety, but there may be things you can do to modify the environment and to partially modify your beliefs and perceptions so the match is sufficiently close so that you can achieve a higher level of emotional well-being. Still, you always have an option. The option of changing your environment or of changing your belief – or a little bit of both.

"Is my belief justified?" You have to ask this question in every situation. The belief that a firm and swift punishment is beneficial may be justified when teaching your children the difference between right and wrong. But that same belief may be totally inappropriate in the office where you may want to encourage others to take the risks required to achieve a new level of profitability.

What Can I Do About It?

No two people will perceive things in exactly the same way. Some people will go to the airport on their day off, look forward to climbing aboard a perfectly functioning airplane, and then leap out of it at 10,000 feet as a member of their skydiving club. However, a person with a phobia of flying will see the air traffic control tower, observe the planes taking off and landing, and may have a full blown panic attack. Exact same stimulus. Totally different response. And clearly what is happening is in the perception.

No two people will perceive things in the same way, and that is because they are never responding to absolute reality. What they are really responding to is an abstraction of reality. You are not responding to these words. What you are responding to is the electrochemical translation of those words into an image in your brain. It is really that image to which you are responding. Furthermore, the image in your brain may be quite different from that of another person. You are going to filter my words through your belief, which, as I have explained, has been influenced by, among other things, the experiences you have had. And few of us have had identical life-experiences so our perceptions of the world will nearly always be different from those of others.

I was surprised to learn this while I was presenting a seminar on the subject of guided imagery and the immune system. Research I had conducted on the subject of guided imagery as a treatment for cancer had resulted in an interview with Diane Sawyer on the CBS television program *60 Minutes*. This national publicity resulted in numerous invitations from around the country to speak on this subject. As always, I presented a balanced viewpoint--speaking about the positive aspects of imagery and, at the same time, speaking about how it can hasten your demise if you are not careful. At the end of the seminar, a lady came up to me and said, "*Dr. Hall, when I had cancer diagnosed, the doctors gave up on me. They said it was too advanced to respond to any of the available treatments and that I had less than 2 years to live. Then I read a book on imagery, which I believed in. It made sense so I tried it. Do you know that that was 6 years ago? I know the imagery saved my life, and I want to thank you for saying all the wonderful things you just said about it.*" A short time later, a man came up and said, "*Dr. Hall, I'm a psychologist in Bethesda. I've always known that guided imagery is a crock, and I just want to tell you that it was very refreshing to hear a scientist who has done research in this area say it is a complete waste of people's time.*"

It was then that I understood the wisdom of the Chinese proverb, "*What the eye sees and what the ear hears is what is already in the mind.*" In other words, we have a tendency to create images that will validate a pre-existing belief. It's analogous to the artist who is contemplating painting a beautiful scene. She sets up her easel, props up the canvas, and takes out her paints. And then she begins to assess the view as to what to put down on that canvas. She soon realizes there must be an airport nearby because, periodically, planes fly across the horizon. But she decides the planes don't belong in this natural setting, so even though they are part of the reality, she doesn't include them. And behind her is a beautiful, weathered cedar tree, which is really not part of the reality. But how it would add to the painting if it were. So the tree is moved to the foreground. It's called artistic license, and we all do it. We have a tendency to delete those things that we do not want to be part of our image, and we include things in our image that were never a part of the original reality. In addition, the image changes over time as we have more experiences, and we get further and further from the actual event. The image becomes a less and less accurate abstraction of what actually happened. It is not that people are deliberately deceiving themselves. NO. They could pass a lie detector test with flying colors. Our mind tends to operate on some sort of belief-driven autopilot.

It's important to recognize that the initial event that gives rise to the emotion is not the image but rather the belief that shapes the information giving rise to that image. Thus, a mismatch between your belief and the circumstances may result in far more than a small amount of artistic license. Now, the image may become so distorted, it drives unhealthy emotions.

The more open-minded you are, the more you read, the more you experience, the more feedback you accept from other people, the more willing you are to listen to alternative viewpoints, then the more information that will go into your image, and the greater the probability that your image will more closely reflect reality. While perception creates the image, beliefs help create the perception. And that's the part you can change.

To determine if your belief is appropriate for the circumstances, ask yourself the seven questions pertaining to beliefs that are listed earlier in this chapter. And make sure you keep asking those questions because the environment can change. So don't just ask those questions once, and then cling to that belief. For example, you can say, "*I cannot do this right now, but, perhaps, if I take classes on the subject, I will acquire the skills I need to achieve this objective.*"
And remember to examine where the belief came from. Is it yours? I told you how my life has been changed by the erroneous belief that no one in my family was any good at learning math. I wonder how many gifted athletes, scientists, and artists are unknown to the world because of a chance statement by a parent or friend proclaiming, "*Oh, you can't possibly make a living doing that,*" and they never even pursued their dream.

Think about it. An African-American girl born into poverty in a small, Southern town in Mississippi, who, at the age of 13, suffered abuse and molestation and became a runaway teenager. What are the chances of her becoming a successful woman who reaches out and helps millions of people every day? What if Oprah Winfrey had failed to do what she knew she could?

Could you have imagined a college dropout who went to Albuquerque, New Mexico, to follow his preposterous dream, who began his business in a cheap motel with hookers next door, would end up the richest man in the world? No erroneous belief stopped Bill Gates.

Who would have thought a gal born in Nutley, New Jersey - a former model turned caterer - would become with a homemaking business an entrepreneur who could rival the likes of Bill Gates? Nothing –not bad advice nor criticism - stopped Martha Stewart.

And, thank goodness, Michael Jordan did not accept the belief of his high school basketball coach in Wilmington, North Carolina. The one who told him that he was not good enough to play basketball. How wonderful that Michael Jordan didn't allow this erroneous belief to keep him from pursuing his dream.

Make sure that you know what your beliefs are. It's the most important step. Many people don't know. Then determine if your belief is based on accurate and complete information. Sometimes we tend to formulate a belief based on only a fragment of the information available to us.

Perhaps I should mention that I happen to be clairvoyant and can peer into the future. I can tell you right now whom you are going to be able to vote for in the next Presidential election. There will be a Democrat, a Republican, and an Independent party candidate. And I know a lot about these candidates, much of which will not be known publicly until after the election. These will be your choices. Candidate number one is a chain smoker, drinks half a dozen martinis throughout the day, and has had two elicit sexual affairs. Candidate number two is also a chain smoker; he sleeps until noon, admits to having smoked opium in college, drinks champagne during the afternoon, and sometimes knocks off a quart of brandy in the evening before going to bed. Candidate number three is a decorated war hero, champions the cause of the common man, drinks an occasional beer, does not smoke, and has never had an illicit sexual affair. Would you be inclined to vote for candidate number one, candidate number two, or candidate number three? Candidate number one was Franklin Roosevelt. Candidate number two, Sir Winston Churchill. And candidate number three, Adolph Hitler.

Sometimes, we have a tendency to make decisions and to formulate a belief based upon only a fragment of the information available to us. And that belief is shaped, in part, by our value system. Some people value certain things so profoundly that unless the person they work with subscribes to exactly the same religion or has exactly the same health habits, they will make no attempt to even meet that individual, when, in fact, that person might enable them to achieve new heights in their profession. Or your neighbor down the street might be your new, potentially best, friend. But because of one characteristic, you may make no attempt to even meet that person.

Occasionally, your intuition pays off, and you should reject a person based upon a tiny fragment of information. More often, however, the greater the amount of information you have, the more options you have in making an informed decision, which will be correct and honest.

A Quick Fix

I've explained ways for dealing with the understanding and eventual changing of your belief. But those techniques won't do you much good during an emergency. When you find yourself in the midst of an emotional crisis, that is not the time to be sitting back and saying, *"What are my beliefs? And is it my belief or somebody else's? What were those seven questions?"* The process I have described is fine for making long-term adjustments; however, occasionally, you need to be able to do something immediately. And one of the most effective ways of putting the brakes on the emotional response and maintaining control so that you can remain focused is to boost your sense of satisfaction.

There's only one thing that is consistently characteristic of a happy person. It's not age, gender, wealth, or health. Happiness is experienced when you are truly satisfied with what you currently have. Be careful. Dissatisfaction is an excellent motivator. You should not be satisfied with things that are within your power to improve. But when you have done your best and are satisfied with your circumstances, then happiness will be the result. Here's a very simple way to improve your levels of satisfaction. Complete this statement three times in the context of whatever is happening:

I am glad I am not _____.

If you find yourself caught in gridlock with no way of making it to the important meeting, complete this statement by saying, *"I am glad I am not a part of the accident that is causing this traffic jam."* Or if your child comes home from school with failing grades, complete this statement by saying, *"I am glad I did not just receive a call from the emergency room regarding my child."* It's called reframing, and it may explain why people who have dealt with a great deal of adversity are often better able to deal with future crises. As a result of having successfully endured and survived a bad situation, they learn that everything is temporary. In the words of the Anglo-Saxon poem *Deor*, "This, too, shall pass." Now, when they find themselves in a quandary, they can reflect upon the previous incident, which will make the current episode seem trivial by comparison.

I was living in Grenada during the Marxist revolution and recall dozens of panic-stricken American medical students seeking any avenue off the island. They even offered local fishermen vast sums to transport them to safety in small, dilapidated boats. Thank goodness that the fishermen declined. There's no way that many of those boats would have safely made the crossing to the next island. On the other hand, the expatriates who resided on the island took it all in stride. One resident had lived through countless revolutions in Africa. Others had lived in London during World War II and had endured the relentless bombings. Their perspective was very different. They had been through far worse and had survived. Therefore, they were confident that they could do so this time.

By reflecting upon a previous experience or by simply imagining something worse, you find yourself becoming more satisfied with your present circumstances. What many people do is just the opposite. They make things worse by completing the statement:

I wish I were_____.

That sequence of words is a recipe for dissatisfaction. *I wish I had a better car, a bigger house, or a more meaningful job* will simply reinforce your perception that you are dissatisfied.

Faith and Optimism

The Russians were preparing to launch the first satellite into space; American advisors were venturing into Vietnam; and

Ruth Fisher was my sixth-grade teacher. Yet, with a stroke of her pen, she had as great an impact on shaping my life as those world events would have on shaping the following decades. *"Nicholas doesn't pay attention. He wastes time, and he fails to follow instructions,"* she wrote on the back of my C- and D-strewn report card. Hardly words of praise, yet they instilled in me a sense of confidence and optimism. The lasting message was conveyed between the words: *"Nicholas doesn't...wastes time...fails to follow instructions."* It was *I* who was in command. My lackluster grades were not the consequence of a low IQ or some genetically-inspired inability to learn. Instead, those D's were the result of my actions—or, rather, lack of actions. At any time, I *chose*; I could have earned A's and B's. All I had to do was start paying attention and start following instructions. That was my choice, and it required no help from anyone.

Pity the poor student who, despite paying attention and following instructions, still failed. Chances are, the teacher would have concluded, *John is just not good at math* or *Mary just doesn't do well on tests.* John and Mary will learn that they have a problem with no clear solution in hand. They are being told that there is a problem with *them.* I was told there was a problem with my *choices.* As a consequence, I came to recognize that most of life's hurdles are temporary setbacks and are capable of being overcome. I learned to be optimistic. Here are some other things I've learned along the way:

- Nothing in life is permanent. While lessons learned early in life can have a lasting impact, pessimism can be changed. The steps are the foundation of cognitive psychology.

- Learn to succeed through failure in the same way many successful CEOs have. Despite being labeled as dyslexic or ADD as children, they found that the problem was not their style but the mismatch with their environment.

- Optimism is realistic, not positive-thinking. It is recognizing that doing something can make a difference. It is no wonder that optimism predicts a reduced incidence of cancer and improved immunity. Optimists also have more friends since they are more fun to be around. Social support is yet another pathway to optimal health.

Clearly, optimism is a trait engrained during early childhood. However, that's water under the bridge. You can't go back and rewrite history. So what are your current options? What steps can you take to instill a sense of optimism long after having a pessimistic explanatory style imposed upon your psyche? There are things you can do, but it won't be easy. That's because it may require reprogramming your brain.

In the face of adversity, you are likely to respond to a threat by engaging in either approach or avoidance behaviors. In the extreme, you would either fight or run away. Associated with the approach system is optimism. It's highly unlikely that you would engage in a behavior unless you anticipated a positive outcome. Enthusiasm and pride would generally occur when moving toward a goal. In contrast, another system is associated with withdrawal from an aversive environment. Negative affect, perhaps in the form of disgust or fear, will generally be associated with putting distance between yourself and the source of the threat. Your tendency to withdraw will keep you from your goal.

Martin Seligman has conducted a number of studies revealing that people's individual coping styles will have an impact on their response to threat. People who recognize that adversity does not have to permeate every aspect of their life, that adversity is temporary, and, largely, the result of external events, have an optimistic explanatory style and, generally, will rebound faster from stress-inducing events. They will view the event as a challenge and engage in approach behaviors. Their attitude is, "*I can do this.*" In contrast, those who personalize events and embrace the belief that every aspect of their life will be negatively and permanently impacted are said to have a pessimistic explanatory style. They tend to view adversity as an obstacle and engage in avoidance behaviors.

Anatomy of Optimism

A specific part of the brain called the prefrontal cortex appears to be partially responsible for determining whether a person will approach or avoid a threat. This bi-lobed structure is located above the orbits at the front of the brain. Different regions of this structure are responsible for shaping your responsiveness to events. The left side contributes to positive feelings since patients with damage to this region are more likely to be depressed. This observation is consistent with electrophysiological data. When healthy people are exposed to emotion-eliciting events, there is increased activity on the left side of the brain during times when the person is experiencing happiness, and there is more activity on the right side of the brain when they are sad.

So often, we tend to think that if something is associated with an event in the brain, it must be the cause of a behavior and not itself subject to behavioral influences. That is not true of the prefrontal lobes. A technique called mindfulness meditation has been shown capable of bringing about not only a change in brain activity but also a change in outlook. It's a technique that requires instruction and practice. Therefore, it is beyond the scope of this book to provide an in-depth description of the protocol. Nonetheless, it involves the induction of a meditative state, while maintaining an awareness of something in the environment. Usually, it is an aroma, a sound, or some other feature, which, otherwise, would not be a part of your conscious awareness.

When taking steps to change your outlook, do not replace pessimism with positive thinking. That is not a feature of optimism. Bad things happen, and, when they do, there may be nothing to justify a rosy outlook. As defined by Seligman, optimism pertains to how you perceive adversity. It's more about non-negative thinking than it is about being positive. Seligman has formulated what he refers to as the ABC technique for replacing a pessimistic explanatory style with one that is optimistic.

- **Adversity**: Identify the problem minus any feelings. It's merely a description of what has happened.
- **Beliefs**: Examine the beliefs that are shaping your response.
- **Consequences**: Reflect upon your actions as well as their consequences.

This is really a modification of cognitive therapy, used extensively by mental health workers. The basic formula, which you will engage in yourself, is as follows:

- Identify the automatic thoughts, which make you feel worse.
- Consider opposite interpretations as you dispute these harmful thoughts.
- Create different explanations.
- Develop a strategy to distract yourself from negative thoughts.
- Examine carefully the depression-inducing beliefs that give rise to your pessimism.

Creating Mental Images

Up until now, I have discussed how your beliefs can shape images triggered by events around you. But do you know that you can create images based upon events within you? These images, in turn, can help you achieve the goals you dream of.

Determine what your image will be. Your favorite vacation spot. A quiet room. A concert hall, beach, or garden. It can be from your past and based upon fact, or it can be a creation of your imagination. Or, perhaps, you'd like to create a mental collage, drifting from one pleasant place to another. If it helps, gaze upon the scene in a picture, and let that be your setting, imagining that you are now a part of it.

Select an object, a fragrance, or a piece of music that will be a part of your image. Make it something unusual, something that you would not normally encounter. This is going to be your 'conditioned stimulus.' By having it present when you create the image, it will acquire similar properties to Pavlov's bell. Except now, you want it to activate the emotions and physiology associated with your imagery session. Later, just by exposing yourself to the object, you will more quickly enter the state you want to be in.

Isolate yourself from distracting, sensory stimuli. Make sure that the room is quiet, that you are comfortable, and that there are no distractions. Include dimensions that will enhance your image. Appropriate music and fragrances may enrich the mood, so let them bath your imagination.

Relax. If your mind is preoccupied with something else, intrusive thoughts will make it difficult for you to create anything except superficial images. Colors, aromas, sounds, and an awareness of small details within the place you have created will only transpire when you are totally relaxed. Take a warm bath. Listen to relaxing music. Read some poetry. Take deep, abdominal breaths. Use progressive muscle relaxation. Do whatever works for you.

Immerse yourself in your journey. Picture the setting from afar, as though you are watching the scene on a large, theater screen. Observe the objects, people, sounds, fragrances, and colors. Is it warm or cold? Identify a place where you would like to be, and move towards it, noting how everything changes with your perspective. Become a part of the scene. Create a scene that warrants a smile. As you take in your surroundings, gently rotate your head in a tension-releasing sweep around your shoulders, observing new things as your head slowly moves.

Practice creating images. Remember, it's your belief-driven image that governs the emotions, which, in turn, are able to impact every aspect of your personal and professional life. If you want to do the things you want to do, you must learn to control your images.

I've described the characteristics of core, cultural, hand-me-down, advertised, and biological beliefs and the questions you should ask to determine if the belief that guides you is the one you really should be embracing. It's important to do this before anything else, for your beliefs impact on virtually every aspect of your life.

BECAUSE I DON'T HAVE TIME

I suffer from a chronic condition, which keeps me in a constant state of turmoil. It's called Optimistic Bias, and it's characterized by the belief that *I can accomplish more than is humanly possible in a given amount of time.* If you suffer from the same malady, here are some things you might try.

Many books have been written on the subject of how to manage your time, and there are numerous seminars that can help you get motivated. In general, the advice is basically the same: you need to have an idea of what needs to be accomplished in a given period of time, and then you need to set priorities.

Use Your Time Efficiently

Everyone needs to have objectives that they want to achieve in order to give their life purpose. Whatever the dream happens to be, it has to be realistic and something you truly want -- not something you are doing just to please other people. Did you know that just thinking about a goal or writing that goal down will help facilitate your accomplishing it? Once you've identified what it is you want to achieve, it becomes easier to identify the information and circumstances that will help you achieve that goal.

Here are the ground rules:

Divide Projects into Manageable Components: Break your goal into smaller and more manageable component parts. The reason is quite simple. When you focus upon the endpoint, it may seem as though the project is overwhelming. If you want to write a book, it may be very difficult getting the motivation to begin because you feel that you couldn't possibly accomplish such a goal. But no one has ever written a book. Instead, people write words, which come together as sentences, which come together as paragraphs, which, in turn, become chapters. It's also a way to organize your time in the most efficient way possible.

Don't Always Set Time Limits: Most of the time, I recommend that you set a time during which you need to accomplish a particular goal. It might be within a certain number of days, weeks, or, perhaps, months. The reason is because setting deadlines provides structure, which many people need. Be careful, though. If you fail to accomplish your goal within that defined time frame, you may end up reinforcing your belief that you are a failure. Set the goal, but impose a time limit only if it is needed to help you maintain focus. Sometimes, it doesn't really matter when you complete the task. Whether your goal is to lose weight or to create a piece of art, you are still a success as long as you are making progress. It may not always work when responding to the demands of your boss; but, if there's no need to impose a time constraint, then why add to your anxiety?

Don't Over-Publicize Your Goal: Some professionals recommend that you tell others about your objectives to provide the additional motivation you might need in order to see the task through to completion. Of course, you want to share your goal with those people who will be affected by it. Furthermore, many people benefit by having a 'buddy' with the same goal. I'm advising against making prominent, public announcements. Why set yourself up for public embarrassment if you fail to accomplish your objective? It's just not necessary. In fact, it may encourage others to badger you, especially if you're trying to lose weight. At the next office party when you reach for that extra piece of cake, you are inviting people to remind you of all the calories you are putting into your mouth. Instead of subjecting yourself to public scrutiny, go about achieving your goal, and wait for others to notice that you've shed a few pounds or that your clothes fit better. That's a much better way to do it.

Dealing with Psychological Barriers: If you are a person who sets a goal, but you never seem to accomplish it, consider the possibility that the reason is not because you don't have the necessary skills to organize your time. Perhaps, instead, you are running into some hand-me-down beliefs. You may have been criticized as a child and told that you were not capable of doing certain things. Or, that you would never amount to anything because every one of your ancestors was totally incompetent when it came to working with their hands, for example. If a parent or some other authority figure instills negative beliefs such as these at an impressionable age, they easily can become self-fulfilling prophesies. Furthermore, beliefs about oneself don't change overnight. Sometimes, the most important, first step in achieving a particular objective is to change the way you see yourself and to start believing that you do have the ability to achieve your dreams.

Do It for Yourself: Make sure that the goal you set is truly your goal and that what you're doing is not intended simply to please someone else. It might please others, but that should not be the primary motivation. I've taught students in medical schools for the past 20 years, and I've lost track of the number of students who really didn't want to be doctors. They were struggling to get good grades and to achieve that objective because it was what their parents wanted. They would reach a certain point in their training, and, suddenly, they would realize that they were not pursuing their own dream, but someone else's. Then, after having invested, maybe, ten years of their life in achieving this goal, they felt stuck with no alternative but to complete it. Recently, a former student who is now a successful doctor contacted me about how to start a new profession as a motivational speaker. Despite all the trappings of success, he can't enjoy life because his goals have been inconsistent with his values. Alternatively, you might define a particular goal because you want to impress a specific group of people. Ironically, those people may not be the least bit concerned about your personal happiness; yet, you are trying to impress them. In the process, you sacrifice your own development as a person.

Be Flexible: When setting about to pursue a dream, be flexible. If you have set life-long goals, then you need to review these at least once a year to see if the goals you felt were important when you were in your 20's are still important to you in your 40's. You may have new responsibilities, health problems, or other considerations that limit what is realistic for you to accomplish. So, on a regular basis, subject your goals to re-assessment in much the same way that you subject your beliefs to re-analysis. Answer these questions:

Are your goals new, or did you formulate them years ago but have yet to achieve them? If the latter, why have you been unable to make more headway?

Do you have too many goals and insufficient time to spend working towards them?

Have you wasted time and effort on objectives that had nothing to do with your lifelong goals?

Are your values mirrored in the steps you take to achieve your objectives?

Reflecting on the answers to these questions will shed considerable light on the changes you might need to make in order to begin making progress. If you don't remove hidden

70

obstacles to achieving your goals, positive steps can be discouragingly slow.

What's Your Optimal Time?

You may have a surplus of energy, but you may not have it at the times you need it. Many people make the mistake of tackling the things that they have to do on the basis of urgency. They fail to take into account that there are times of the day when they are better able to take on certain types of tasks as opposed to others. As the sun progresses from the Eastern horizon to the West, so are our bodies changing. When we first get up in the morning, we have a large amount of the chemical that mobilizes energy. This chemical is called cortisol; and, as the day goes on, the levels gradually drop, bottoming out at about 3:00 in the morning, a time when most people normally are asleep. It then rises when we get out of bed, providing us with the energy we need to make it through the day. There are also ultradian rhythms. As opposed to a circadian rhythm, which means *about the day*, ultradian rhythms mean *within the day*. One of the best characterizations is the constant shifting in brain dominance.

You've undoubtedly heard of the left versus right-brain. The left-brain is primarily responsible for language and analytical skills. The right-brain, however, is involved more with artistic pursuits. Creating sculptures, music awareness, and music expression depend more upon neurons based in the right hemisphere. Every 90 to 110 minutes, you switch. For part of the day, the electrical activity on one side of the brain is more pronounced than it is on the other. Have you ever found yourself in the middle of a task, where you are in what psychologists would refer to as 'flow' or, in athletics, 'the zone'? You are doing what you need to do almost effortlessly, and it seems as though you could go on forever. Your performance is flawless. The clay is literally coming to life in

71

your hands as you create the piece of art. But, then you take a short break. You return to the task, and now the clay literally crumbles in your hands. Or, the report that you had been writing with very little effort now is impossible to resume. A contributing factor could very well be that you have switched from the side of the brain that would facilitate accomplishing this task. Writing a report depends upon language. That's a left-brain function, while creating a sculpture would require the right.

What you need to do is select the time of day when you are most likely to be able to complete the task at hand. If it requires a certain amount of energy and physical exertion, then select a time of day when your glucocorticoids will be elevated, for example, the morning. If it's a language-based task, then select a time of day when you are more likely to be in your left-hemisphere as opposed to your right. No, you do not need sophisticated electronic equipment to determine in which side of the brain you are operating. You very well may be able to determine this by doing the following nasal exercise.

Take a deep breath through your nose. Now do it again, and pay attention through which nostril you are breathing. Obviously, you are probably breathing through both simultaneously; but, if you pay very careful attention, you'll notice that the air is passing more readily through one side as opposed to the other. What facilitates the passage of air is constriction of blood vessels on that side. The more constricted the blood vessels, the more readily air will pass through the corresponding nostril. Vascular constriction is controlled by the autonomic nervous system. Unlike other components of the nervous system, the autonomic nervous system does not cross over. What's happening on one side of your body is happening in the same side of your brain. If the air is passing more readily through your left nostril, that means that the blood vessels are not only maximally constricted in your left nostril, but they are also maximally constricted in the

72

left side of your brain. There's going to be relatively more blood flow in the opposite hemisphere. What is the translation of this information? Quite simply, you are in the side of the brain opposite to the nostril that you are breathing through. Just as your electrical activity shifts from one side of the brain to the other in an ultradian type of fashion, so does the ease with which air passes through your nostrils. After you have established which nostril you are breathing through most readily, try it again in about an hour. Chances are, you will have switched.

I realize that this sounds like a rather unscientific approach, but the phenomenon is real. You cannot dispute data, just their interpretation. A number of studies have documented that the switch from the left side to the right does, indeed, occur. Whether it is due to subtle changes in vasoconstriction is not absolutely clear. Regardless of the mechanism whereby the switch is taking place, the fact that changes in the brain occur has been known since antiquity in India. Hunters recognized that there were certain times during the day when they were less likely to be successful as compared with others. They determined when that time of day was on the basis of which nostril they were breathing through.

It's 10:00 AM; and at 11:00 AM, you have to have a very important report on your supervisor's desk. You have just switched over, and you are now breathing through your left nostril, which means, of course, that you are in your right-brain. This is not the best side of the brain to be in if you want to achieve flow while writing a report. You need to be in your left-brain, which is where language is based; and that, in turn, means that you should be breathing more readily through your right nostril. Some people claim to be able to shift their dominance by forcing themselves to breathe through the nostril that they need to be breathing through. By holding your nostril and forcing yourself to breathe through one or the other, it is possible to shift the dominance profile. There are

73

even a few scientific papers documenting that this can be achieved under laboratory conditions, as well. Whether it will work for you is something that you will have to find out.

Sex Rhythms

Much has been written about the tidal-like movement of estrogen and progesterone, which gives rise to physiological and, sometimes, mood changes in pre-menopausal women. But men experience changes associated with fluctuations in testosterone. They can influence performance and feelings on a daily, monthly, annual, and lifetime basis. Coaches and athletes are certainly aware of this. Even in the absence of any identifiable factor, there are times when athletes drop into a performance slump. Most likely, it is due to changes in the anabolic steroid, testosterone. This classic male hormone not only drops the voice an octave or two, but it also can be converted into estrogen. Thus, men also may be subject to mood changes.

Testosterone can fluctuate during the day. It's normally highest in the morning and then drops at around bedtime. Superimposed upon this diurnal rhythm are mini-cycles that take place over a period of 15 to 20 minutes – approximately the interval that some men claim to fantasize about sex. Levels are also more likely to be higher during the fall and prior to the age of 40. Afterwards, there's an approximately 10 percent decline with each, subsequent decade. Of course, levels of stress, exercise, and diet may impact the rate of change. For some men, these variations may be so subtle as to be inconsequential. For others, they may explain noticeable changes in both mental and physical abilities. How can you find out? Try this:

Keep a detailed diary. Record everything that happens pertinent to what you want to accomplish. Do you want to find out why you zone out every day between 3:00 PM and 4:00 PM? Or how you can anticipate in advance those moments when everything you do works out just the way you wanted? Are you in a certain state because of conditioning? Are hormones running the show? You need to track everything, especially diet and time of day. Any rhythmicity would suggest a biological factor. If something happens seemingly at random or correlated only with certain events, chances are it's an environmentally-induced phenomenon. Eventually, you will study each page to determine if there are any consistent correlations. Then, using these data, pick the optimal time to do those things you need to accomplish.

BECAUSE I DON'T HAVE THE ENERGY

The Problem

Unless you have sufficient energy, you'll lack both the will and the ability to achieve your goals. There is probably no greater barrier to physical and emotional well-being than fatigue. Failure to get a good night's sleep is invariably the problem - and it is a costly one. The sleep debt in the United States makes the economic debt look trivial by comparison.

Over 40 million Americans suffer from sleep disorders. More than 200,000 traffic accidents occur each year because of driver fatigue, and lack of sleep is the cause of 33% of fatal truck accidents. Studies at Stanford University have revealed that drowsy drivers are actually more impaired than most drunken drivers. All totaled, the direct and indirect costs resulting from sleep disorders and fatigue may be as much as $116 billion a year. It's time to start viewing chronic, insufficient rest as a physical disability. It's imperative that you take steps to deal with it. If you don't, you won't be able to do the things you want because you can't.

The Top Causes of Fatigue

- Too much work and not enough recreation
- Iron deficiency
- Sleep apnea
- Depression
- Emotional loss
- Thyroid problems
- Recent illness
- Snoring partners
- Sedentary lifestyle

The Solution

There is also a serious problem in that most people's circadian rhythms run faster than society's clocks. Many internal, biological clocks are on a 26-hour cycle, while the world operates on a 24-hour day. There are things you can do, though, to reset your internal clock. Expose yourself to sunlight as soon as possible after rising. Light signals the brain to set most of the body's biological clocks. If you suspect a medical cause, then guidance from a health care professional is clearly warranted. Otherwise, consider doing some of the following:

Get low impact exercise early in the day. It stimulates your mind plus sets in motion a series of physiological events that result in your body gradually slowing down over the course of the day.

Get out of bed if you haven't fallen asleep within 20 minutes. Lying there worrying about not being able to sleep only protracts the problem. Do something boring - C-SPAN and local government access cable channels are excellent to watch, or read one of those dry trade journals you've brought home from work.

Relax. Use progressive muscle relaxation exercises, deep breathing, or simply count sheep. By concentrating on such efforts, you block troublesome thoughts, which can keep you awake.

Drink a glass of warm milk. Yes, mother was right. We now know why. Milk contains an amino acid, which creates a chemical chain reaction in the brain that helps induce sleep. But, if you suffer from indigestion or acid reflux, milk can actually intensify such gastric discomforts. Experiment to see if this is an option.

Watch what you eat. Fatigue may be due to eating the wrong foods. Studies have shown that approximately two hours after consuming a meal rich in carbohydrates, you will experience fatigue as well as impaired performance on tests requiring speed and concentration. That's because the consumption of carbohydrates facilitates the transport of tryptophan into the brain. The more tryptophan that gets into the brain, the more there is available to be converted into serotonin, a neurotransmitter that stimulates sleep. Timing is everything. Save carbohydrates for dinner, not for the lunch you might consume a couple of hours before having to go into a high-powered, demanding meeting.

Get something hot. There are health benefits associated with ingesting hot peppers and sauces that contain capsaicin, which imparts the hot flavor. But don't have a snack with Tabasco sauce just before you go to bed; it may trigger indigestion. That might be what's waking you up in the middle of the night.

Smoking cigarettes can disrupt your sleep cycle. Carbon monoxide, which is found in tobacco smoke, can interfere with the ability of red blood cells to transport oxygen throughout the body. The less oxygen you have, the less energy you're going to have. Smoking also can impede blood flow and the transport of oxygen by triggering the accumulation of mucous in both the windpipe and the bronchial tubes. This, in turn, will constrict blood vessels and the oxygenation of cells in the body.

Avoid caffeine, especially after about 5:00 in the afternoon, and remember there is as much caffeine in a can of cola as there is in half an average cup of coffee. Perhaps, you were able to get away with drinking huge amounts of this and other caffeine-containing beverages when you were younger. But, as you age and your metabolism slows, it's going to take longer for the body to break the caffeine into its various metabolites. Therefore, the caffeine will remain in your system for a longer period of time. Just because you were able to get away with drinking large amounts of coffee as a student, don't be surprised if those old habits are associated with some consequences later in life.

Stay away from sleeping pills. The benzodiazepines and barbiturates are addictive, and eventually you'll have no choice but to take these medications if you're going to get any sleep at all. You also should avoid nightcaps. One national survey reports that 29% of people who report difficulty sleeping rely upon alcohol in order to induce a state of relaxation. There's no question that alcohol will induce a state of sleep, but the quality of the sleep you get is lowered, and it's almost guaranteed that you will be prone to waking up, usually about four to five hours after you fall asleep. Alcohol also can impair your ability to take in oxygen. It causes over-relaxation of the muscles and inhibits the respiratory system. The net result is a reduction in your ability to breathe efficiently. All of these things reduce levels of energy.

Create a diversion. There are lots of things you can do to divert yourself, so find a technique that you feel comfortable with and use it. Whatever you do, do it vividly. If you are counting sheep, then visualize each sheep in your mind in order to block intrusive thoughts. Concentrate on your body relaxing, and chances are you won't even recall what number you got to before you fell asleep. You also can count your blessings, adding a sense of joy or gratitude to your relaxation.

There is nothing wrong with healthy worrying. It's only when the worrying interferes with sleep or other functions you have to perform. Set aside time to worry some time before you go to bed. Get it out of your system. While you are doing this, think about what it is you're going to do the next day. List the most important tasks you need to accomplish, so that when you awaken, you'll know exactly what needs to be done. And don't do your worrying in bed or in your favorite chair. Otherwise, the bed will trigger worrying, just as Pavlov's bell triggered salivation in dogs.

Turn the clock. Don't have your clock staring at you next to the bed, so that every time you open your eyes, you are aware of how late it is and the fact that you are still not asleep. Turn it so that you have to expend some effort in order to see what time it is.

Cool down. What enables you to fall asleep is a subtle drop in body temperature. You can fool your body into activating processes that lower your temperature by jumping into a hot tub or taking a hot bath about an hour before you are ready for bed. The brain will be fooled into thinking you are in danger of dying from hyperthermia. Consequently, it activates processes designed to lower your body temperature sufficiently to compensate for the extra heat. When you leave the source of heat, those processes continue to work, so your body temperature actually drops below normal. You'll have to experiment to determine exactly how long, in advance, you need to do this. Exercise also will work. When you exercise, you temporarily increase your core body temperature. Just make certain that you work out early in the evening so that your body has a chance to cool down and to enter into that over-compensation stage at the time you want to sleep.

Exercise. If you are a man in your 50's, you might be waking in the middle of the night to go to the bathroom. As men age, the prostate gland can swell and partially block the urethra. This triggers the need for frequent urination.

81

Obviously, if you cut back on fluid intake before going to bed, this will help; however, a small amount of light exercise an hour before bedtime will work as well. Don't do anything aerobic, simply some very easy, stretching exercises or a short, five-minute walk. This will stimulate the circulation of fluids through the kidneys, and it will prompt you to get rid of a little more fluid before you go to bed.

Establish a sleep pattern, and make sure that you stay with it. Sleep is one of the easiest things to condition in humans. If you train your body to get used to falling asleep at a certain time of night, it's more likely to happen.

CAUTION

Realize that sleep disorders and fatigue may be secondary to an illness, which cannot be regulated through behavior or supplements. For that reason, it is important to have a thorough physical examination to rule out such a cause.

Even after a restful night's sleep, you still need to maintain the energy with which you awakened. That's best done with the right food. Since food is the fuel of the body, you'd think that with more, you'd be able to go further and last longer. To a certain extent, that is true. The average person needs between about 1500 and 2000 calories per day to keep the body going and to make it through the workday. However, more is less important than type and time when it comes to having energy. Lack of energy is what erodes your motivation and keeps you from doing what you want to do. Ask an athlete about 'hitting the wall' or 'bonking.' These expressions refer to the almost total collapse of the body, usually at a point midway through a long-endurance event. Blood sugar drops, and the athlete's energy level bottoms out. It can happen to anyone, though, and will if you eat too much or too little, at the wrong time of day, or in the wrong proportions of protein, carbohydrate, and fat. The following tips are the ones that many endurance athletes use. If the guidelines work for people who push their physical limits for hours on end, imagine what they could do for you.

Graze. Instead of eating three square meals a day, as prescribed by our culture, eat five or six meals of roughly 200 to 300 calories each. When you eat a larger amount, the extra will trigger a surge of insulin in order to place the excess energy into storage. That alone is not a problem. But, it becomes one when you consume large numbers of calories, especially in the form of a high glycemic index food such as rice. Because these foods are more rapidly converted into blood sugar, the rise is quite abrupt. This, in turn, prompts the pancreas to produce a bit too much insulin, causing more sugar than intended to go into storage. Remember the sluggish feeling you experience after a big meal? Now you know why. Another way to trigger excess insulin and the same drop in blood sugar is to eat a candy bar. While not a guaranteed solution, a good place to start is by spreading the calories you need over 6 smaller meals instead of the traditional 3. Now your blood sugar will be more constant during the day since you are eliminating the need for an insulin surge and a subsequent drop. You'll also be less likely to overeat.

Consume Adequate Protein. The more muscle you have, the more calories you burn without doing anything. That's one of the reasons people who are lean and have lots of muscle can get away with eating large portions without gaining excess weight. Building muscle requires adequate protein in your diet. There's considerable information about the amount of protein you should consume relative to carbohydrate, and there's no telling what the latest fad will call for at the time you are reading this. Instead of worrying about percentage of intake, determine your ideal weight and then make sure you consume one gram of protein for each pound of ideal body weight you are striving toward. This is the recommended amount for active people whose ranks you are, hopefully, about to join. If you take up bodybuilding or start running marathons, you may need more. You need protein for everything from muscle to immune system antibodies. Many brain chemicals are also made from the amino acids you get from protein. Foods such as milk, cheese, eggs, poultry, red meat, and fish are good sources of protein. That's why I always take high protein energy bars with me when training and racing. I also take some that are high in carbohydrates when I need a quick energy boost.

Understand Different Types of Carbohydrates. Carbohydrates contain four calories per gram and are the main energy source for the body. When three or more 6-carbon sugar molecules are joined, the resulting molecule is known as a complex carbohydrate. One or two 6-carbon sugar molecules linked together comprise a simple sugar. Complex carbohydrates are further sub-classified into fibrous and starchy carbohydrates. When consumed, simple sugars, like sucrose and dextrose, as well as refined complex carbohydrates, like white flour, provide a burst of energy that often gives way to feelings of lethargy. Typically, unrefined complex carbohydrates are assimilated by the system more slowly than simple sugars and will provide constant and sustained (though less intense) energy levels.

Limit Sugars in Favor of Low Glycemic Index Carbohydrates. The lower the glycemic index of a given carbohydrate, the more gradually it will be digested into its component parts and absorbed from the GI tract into the bloodstream. Less insulin is released from the pancreas over a given time in response to foods with low glycemic indices. Hence, the body has more time to utilize the molecules for fuel, rather than storing them as fat.

Consume Adequate Fiber. Because the human gastrointestinal (GI) tract cannot digest fiber, it does not contribute calories and is passed as waste. It is, nonetheless, vital to good health. Inadequate dietary fiber leads to a sluggish GI tract, water retention, bloating, constipation, and an increased risk of developing colon cancer. In addition to being rich in vitamins, minerals, and antioxidants, fruits and leafy vegetables are excellent fiber sources, and most experts advise consuming at least five servings per day. For optimal fat burning, limit starchy carbohydrate consumption later in the day, eating plenty of fresh fruits and vegetables, instead.

Eat a Low-Fat Diet. Fats contain 9 calories per gram, more than twice the amount found in carbohydrates and proteins. Saturated fats, derived from animal sources, have been shown to contribute more heavily to the development of cardiovascular disease than unsaturated fats, derived from plant sources. For health reasons, fats should be limited to less than 20% of total, consumed calories.

Drink A Lot of Water. Many nutritionists recommend that the active individual consume a minimum of one gallon of water per day, although that will vary depending upon your level of activity and the weather. Water aids the liver and kidneys in the detoxification of poisons and in the elimination of wastes from the body. Without sufficient water, we become dehydrated, and our organs (including muscle, liver, and kidney) do not function optimally. Optimal kidney function leaves the liver free to perform maximum lypolysis, or fat burning. In addition, water is both an appetite suppressant as well as an excellent diuretic. Not only will high fluid intake increase urination, it also will decrease overall water retention. Although you may have to work up to a gallon a day gradually over a week or so while your bladder adjusts, you will reap the benefits of your efforts almost immediately. In fact, drinking water below your body temperature can actually help you to lose weight. Did you know that consuming one gallon of water chilled to 4 degrees

Fahrenheit could cause your body to liberate over 150 calories of energy? What an easy way to burn fat! Of course if you are running low on energy, this practice could, theoretically, make you even more lethargic, but probably not as much as the extra weight you are carrying. Therefore, I wouldn't be concerned about this issue.

Aim to Prevent, Not Quench, Your Thirst. Proper hydration leads to enhanced thermo-regulation and increased oxygen exchange in the lungs. Simply stated, the well-hydrated individual will have greater endurance and a more comfortable workout. Since we do not feel thirsty until we are already in a dehydrated state, it is best to drink water with sufficient frequency to prevent thirst.

Eliminate Alcohol. Alcohol is not exactly classified as a nutrient, but it is widely consumed and warrants mention. Alcohol is the enemy of the dieter and the athlete. It contains 7 calories per gram, nearly as much as fat, and is completely without nutritional value. Not only does alcohol contribute empty calories, it slows the body's metabolic rate so that fewer calories are burned over time. In addition, alcohol consumption leads to a transient hypoglycemic state and subsequent food cravings. Finally, alcohol is hepatotoxic, and even moderate drinking can result in fatty deposits on the liver. While the liver works hard to detoxify the system of alcohol, it is less efficient at lipolysis, or fat burning.

Keep Track. Use a book or other guide to keep track of your total calorie consumption as well as your intake proportion of carbohydrates, protein, and fat. You should measure your food (with a measuring cup or scale) until you have a good idea of exactly what a portion actually represents. Most people overestimate portion size and, hence, underestimate their caloric intake. Some of the best resources are those published by the American Dietetic Association.

BECAUSE I'M TOO EMOTIONAL

Emotions are the link between your beliefs and how you conduct your life. They are the link with your immune system and memory as well as your cardiovascular and endocrine systems. Even your reaction time and ability to perform are associated with emotions. Emotions can impede your progress or motivate you to achieve new heights. For instance, sadness can preoccupy you, or it can prompt you to change your circumstances. Fear may paralyze you, or it can prompt you to take precautionary steps, which, in turn, may save your life. Emotions are a double-edged sword. Without them, your life would be dull and meaningless. But too much of a good thing, especially at the wrong time, can derail you.

What Are Emotions?

First and foremost, you should recognize that *emotions are really nothing more than a sensory system. They are the eyes and ears of your body... gauges of your biology.* The brain is a huge endocrine gland that secretes behavior and emotions. The emotions and behavior that are excreted have a biological basis. But it's not like putting a dipstick into the motor of your car to see what the oil level happens to be. You can't put your finger in your ear or up your nose, and then look at it to measure the amount of acetylcholine, norepinephrine, or serotonin in your brain. More often than not, the negative emotions reflect the perception of unmet needs; there is a problem which gives rise to anger or fear. But it's very important to realize that the emotion itself is not the problem. Emotions are nothing more than symptoms or indicators of a problem.

Many people make the mistake of believing that the emotion is the problem. They go to the bookstore and purchase a volume proclaiming to have the solution for vanquishing your anger or for reducing your fear. That's all well and good. By all means, take steps to reduce the anger or the fear that impedes your productivity or blocks your capacity for pleasure. However, at the same time, recognize that if all you do is put a pharmacological or behavioral Band-Aid on the emotion, the problem that led to that emotion will resurface at some other time, perhaps in the form of a derailed immune system, or, possibly, in the form of intestinal upset, skin disease, memory loss, or heart problems. There are a wide number of illnesses that will more readily occur when your body has been altered by emotional upheaval. These now become the answer to the question: *I know what to do, so why can't I do it?*

There are no fewer than 558 words in the English language alone that have emotional connotations. Some people consider all of these 558 words to be individual emotions. Of course, that gets a bit unwieldy. In contrast, the British philosopher John Locke argued that there are really only two emotions: those that give rise to pain and those that give rise to pleasure. The negative emotions are those that are associated with a threat or with the blocking of a goal. The positive emotions, on the other hand, are associated with making progress toward a goal. Is it that simple? Are emotions just good or bad? Is it really that clear-cut? What do you believe?

The ancient Greeks would have argued that all emotions are good; that the ability to express virtually every emotion is essential for the good life. A counterpoint was promoted by the Stoics, who argued that it was a waste of time to experience emotions, especially joy and love, which were considered frivolous. And you can't blame them. Life was absolutely chaotic during that era in ancient history. It really was a waste of time to be joyful because there was so little about which to be joyful. The belief that emotions are inherently bad was driven home during the Middle Ages. Realize that at that time, they didn't use the word *emotion*. Instead, the word *passion* was used. Nonetheless, passion, or, what today we would call emotion, was very closely intertwined with sin, focusing on words like *greed, lust,* and *envy.* To this day, this historical perspective has influenced our cultural beliefs concerning emotions. Despite evidence to the contrary, emotions often are believed to be inherently bad, which may be why many people deny or repress them.

You've heard the expressions - you've probably used them yourself: *Don't be so emotional. Chill out. Be more reasonable.* The implication is that emotions are the opposite of reason; that if you express the emotions that you have, somehow, you have lost control. Not only is this a cultural belief; it may be a hand-me-down belief, as well. It may well explain the reluctance of some people, especially men in Western society, to express their feelings.

Why do some people avoid emotions? People do things for one of two reasons: to avoid pain or to experience pleasure. If a child has a traumatic experience as a result of being punished for expressing anger, she will associate anger with pain, and it will be avoided. If a boy is brought up in an environment where he is taught that the male is the one who always should be strong and in charge, the experience and expression of fear may erode that self-image. So the emotion and the circumstances that might give rise to it are avoided.

In many instances, if you are uncomfortable with the expression of a certain emotion, you may very well align yourself with an individual who also feels uncomfortable with expressing the same emotion. Whether in the workplace or in the family, you reinforce each other and behave in a way that each of you feels comfortable with by avoiding the same emotion.

In other cases, opposites may attract. You may be drawn to a person who is able to express an emotion that you feel uncomfortable with because it makes you feel complete. In other words, opposites both attract and repel, depending upon the circumstances. It can end up being a very stable relationship, but it also has the potential to be very dull and boring, especially when implied mutual consent banishes certain emotions from the relationship.

A few years ago, I was asked to present a lecture on the subject *The Power of Positive Emotions*. It was only a 30-minute talk. But I spent more time working on that 30-minute lecture than I often put into a multi-day program for a large corporation. And there were two reasons for this: the person presenting before me was Richard Simmons, and the person coming on stage immediately after me was Naomi Judd. I was well aware that nobody cared about me. They had no idea who I was. They had virtually no interest in what I had to say. I had been hired by the organizers of a large health fair to bridge the gap between this light-hearted, 'fun' presentation of Simmons, cavorting about the stage in his pink and white shorts and tank top, and the very serious, spiritual message of Naomi Judd. The organizers estimated that it would take about 30 minutes to change the set – and my job was to keep the audience entertained in the meantime.

Actually, that was not really the problem. That was a challenge and, I might add, fun to deal with. The real difficulty was trying to decide which emotions belonged in the positive column and which in the negative column. I couldn't figure it out. Oh, I read the same books you've probably read, but I couldn't agree with the authors. And then one morning when I was out riding my bicycle, I had one of those 'Aha' moments. It suddenly dawned on me that there is no such thing as a positive emotion. All emotions are negative. And then I realized that there are no negative emotions. They are all positive. It is not the emotion that is positive or negative. It is the context in which it arises. It is the match between the emotion and the circumstance that determines whether the same emotion can now have survival value or whether it will be destructive to your health. Let's consider a couple of examples.

Anger is very often placed in the negative column, which it most certainly is when that anger is repressed, or when the anger, which should be expressed to a co-worker or supervisor in the work-place, is taken home and misdirected at your children or your spouse. Yes, that anger is then a very negative emotion. But, if you use anger to motivate you to identify the underlying, unmet need or problem, and, if you express anger in an appropriate way, that anger becomes a virtue, not a vice.

Conversely, the emotion of love is routinely placed in the positive column, which it most certainly is when directed at your children, parents, or your spouse. But, when that same emotion of love is now directed at the spouse of your next-door neighbor, it becomes a very negative, destructive emotion. So is the expression of love that you find depicted in many Valentine's Day cards, the ones that proclaim, *"I couldn't live without you." "I love you so much that my life would not be complete if you were not a part of it."* This, I believe, is a very sick, co-dependent type of love, which fails to provide the individuals in the relationship the opportunity to grow. If you delve into history and literature, you discover that what happened to Romeo and Juliet was the rule, not the exception. That kind of dependent love gets people imprisoned in castles, run over by trains, and murdered - that's if they don't commit suicide first.

The same is true of your beliefs. There is no such thing as a good or bad belief. It is only when a belief is not justified under a particular set of circumstances that it becomes bad. So, like the emotions that they can give rise to, it is the match between a belief and the environment that has to be examined. Even though beliefs and emotions are distinct entities, realize that the belief gives rise to an emotion, which, in turn, communicates through chemicals with the rest of the body. Thus, when you change a belief, it will most likely evoke simultaneous changes in your emotional well-being, your body chemistry, and your health. Through the examination of your beliefs, you can take control and make progress toward achieving your dreams.

When the Blues Set In

At various times, we all experience what is usually described as 'the blues.' When present, it's difficult, if not impossible, to do what you know you should. The treatment of these minor, sub-clinical depressions should focus initially upon determining to what degree environmental factors are responsible for the symptoms. While 'the blues' can progress to major depression, there are vast differences between these two conditions. Clinical or major depressions are generally defined as those due to a biochemical disturbance within the brain.

A number of psychological disorders can be directly linked with chronic stress, although depression is one of the more common consequences. Up to 10% of the population will suffer from a major depression at some point during their lives. It is important to recognize that there are many types of depression. Reactive depression is a response to something about which you are appropriately upset, such as the loss of a job or the loss of a loved one. Or, the depression may be caused by factors, which aren't readily apparent. Bipolar depression is characterized by negative emotions alternating with periods of mania. There is also schizoaffective disorder, during which symptoms of schizophrenia and depression are interspersed.

One of the neurotransmitters that has been implicated in depression is norepinephrine. The evidence linking this transmitter with negative affect is based upon studies showing that drugs capable of elevating this chemical within the body also alleviate the symptoms of depression. There also is evidence suggesting that there might be a genetic deficiency of the enzyme that produces norepinephrine. But, there has to be something that triggers the initial change in the norepinephrine. That trigger is often an environmental stressor. Problems do not arise as long as the susceptible person is not subjected to an event that causes the initial decrease in norepinephrine. Difficulties arise when the norepinephrine becomes depleted through chronic stress, and the neurons cannot produce adequate amounts to compensate. In other words, supply fails to keep pace with demand.

Norepinephrine is not the only neurotransmitter linked with depression. One of the most popular classes of drugs now used in treating depression is selective serotonin re-uptake inhibitors, indicating that this chemical is involved, as well.

Major depression can be recognized through several, unrelenting symptoms, including:

- Overwhelming fatigue
- Impaired concentration
- Impaired memory
- Feelings of worthlessness
- Feeling overwhelmed
- Increase or decrease in appetite
- Changes in sleep behavior
- Decreased ability to experience pleasure

It is important to realize that many of these same symptoms can occur as a consequence of a number of other illnesses unrelated to a chemical imbalance within the brain. Pancreatic cancer, dysfunction of the thyroid gland, as well as a deficiency in cortisol production may all result in such symptoms. A change in diet, regular exercise, and psychotherapy can each help in alleviating the symptoms of depression. But, when such efforts produce no positive effects, it is important to seek medical intervention to determine the underlying cause and proper treatment.

Seeking Counseling or Psychotherapy

Psychotherapy or counseling may be helpful for individuals suffering from an array of emotional difficulties. Individuals suffering from depression, anxiety, relationship problems, eating disorders, panic attacks, phobias, or addictions may benefit from the many treatment approaches that psychologists, social workers, religious leaders, and counselors offer. In addition, therapy can be of great benefit in dealing with stressful events and major life transitions. These may include, for example, job or relationship loss, parenting issues, stress-related illness and physical symptoms, or death and grief. Therapy can often help people adjust more quickly and effectively to adverse events.

In general, when emotional issues begin to interfere with individual, family, work, or social functioning, therapy is indicated. In addition, treatment is clearly indicated for those who are experiencing recurrent thoughts of harming themselves or others, and/or become unable to care for their basic needs. Individuals who need therapy are often caught in a vicious cycle in which their efforts to bring about personal change on their own are increasingly ineffective. In spite of their many attempts to change, people often find that they lack the tools to make changes. In essence, they need the objective perspective of a trained professional. While there are many different treatment approaches, most therapies provide an opportunity to identify ineffective coping patterns and assistance in learning new, more effective methods of responding in a safe, accepting, and supportive environment. Ultimately, a more objective perspective of oneself is gained, and important decisions in life are made more consciously. In short, therapy can help you find the answers.

Seven Ways to Deal with Emotional Turmoil

1. Translate your emotions into language. Talk out loud or simply write the problem down. This will enable you to view the problem through a different sensory modality, for example, the auditory or visual system, giving you a different perspective from which to identify causes and/or solutions.

2. Identify the emotion you are experiencing. Are you feeling sad, angry, fearful, guilty, embarrassed, or a combination of these or others?

3. Identify the source of the problematic emotion. Are you angry with yourself for not accomplishing a goal? Are you fearful or sad about the consequences for not having done so? Are you feeling guilty because you failed? And remember that what really causes you to blow up at the end of the day may very well be some event you've been mulling over all day long.

4. Identify the negative thoughts you might be experiencing and hold them up to reality.

5. Identify those thoughts, which are grossly exaggerated and replace them with more rational thoughts. For example, if you happen to be late for a family gathering, don't assume your family will think that you don't love them. Recognize that they will probably accept that your tardiness was due to reasons outside of your control.

6. Re-think the entire scenario. Just as a result of going through the steps at this point, you probably have already avoided a major, emotional crisis.

7. Once you figure out what went wrong, take corrective action. Learn from your mistakes, and set about to make sure that it doesn't happen again. Remember that even your biggest blunder can always serve as a bad example for future choices.

When Panic Attacks

There are some individuals who experience very intense, physiological symptoms that will occur repeatedly and quite unexpectedly in the absence of any apparent, external trigger. These are referred to as panic attacks, and they are thought to occur when the body's normal stress circuitry becomes inappropriately aroused. Some or all of the following symptoms may accompany these episodes.

There may be an impending fear of dying, a concern about totally losing physical or emotional control, going crazy, or doing something embarrassing. Some people lose their sense of reality, experience flushes or chills, and/or tingling or numbness in the hands. Other individuals experience difficulty breathing, dizziness, chest pains, as well as a racing or pounding heartbeat. Perhaps the best way to describe these attacks is with the word 'terror.' There is a sense that something unimaginably horrible is about to occur and that they have no power to prevent it.

So severe are these attacks that, in many individuals, it is the anxiety associated with the possibility of having another panic attack that, in turn, serves as a trigger for emotional upheaval. The initial panic attack may often be associated with some form of stress. It may result from being overworked, or it may be secondary to the loss of a close family member or friend. Some people experience the attacks following the stress associated with surgery, a serious accident, illness, or even childbirth. Certain drugs also can stimulate panic attacks, for example, excessive consumption of caffeine or the use of cocaine can sometimes trigger these types of reactions. Despite the association with stress, these attacks usually take people totally by surprise, and it is their unpredictable nature that results in their being so disruptive. Obviously, a preoccupation with such disruptive events will stifle any motivation to proceed toward a goal. Here are several strategies for coping with panic, and these will be worthwhile, whether the panic attacks occur intermittently or on a regular basis. You will notice that the strategies are simply modifications of the techniques that already have been described in the context of lesser reactions to stress.

It is important to remember that, although they may seem to be overwhelming, your feelings are not, by themselves, dangerous or harmful.

Know that if you are experiencing a panic attack, you are experiencing the very same physiological changes that evolved to enable you to survive an emergency. You are simply experiencing an exaggeration of your normal response to stress.

Don't try to force the feelings away. The more you are willing to recognize the feelings and face them head-on, the less intense they will become.

Avoid exacerbating your attack by dwelling on what might happen now or in the future.

Maintain a constant flow of calming and affirming self-talk. Remind yourself that you are in no real, physical danger; that you've gotten through this before, and you will survive it again; that the physical symptoms will pass, and it is safe to relax.

Breathe, slowly and deeply, from your diaphragm. This promotes the relaxation response in the body, as well as serves as evidence that you are, indeed, able to breathe just fine.

You might try quantifying your level of fear. Assign a number from 1 to 5, with 5 corresponding to the most intense feelings of fear that you might experience and 1 being minimal intensity. Then rate yourself. What you will observe is that your feelings of anxiety do not remain constant. Instead, they fluctuate. And they'll stay at a very high level for only a few seconds at a time.

Distract yourself. Shifting your attention to a repetitive task may divert your attention and your anxiety.

By utilizing these strategies, you will notice that when you stop engaging in behaviors that add to your fear, the anxiety itself will begin to fade away. You also will become instantly aware that these strategies do work, and this will make you feel good about the fact that you have succeeded. Once you acquire this understanding, you will be ready to successfully achieve your goals.

Overcoming Fear

It's now time to learn some skills to help you better handle negative emotions. Many people cling to outmoded beliefs because they enable them to avoid an emotion that causes pain or discomfort. For example, *Complaining gets you nowhere.* Let's imagine that this belief has its roots in early childhood when a complaint triggered a belligerent reaction on the part of a parent. (For example, Dad believed children should be seen and not heard.) Yes, in that environment and at that time, the child's belief was justified. It kept the kid out of trouble in the home. The fear response elicited by the parent's angry outburst had definite survival value. But, things have changed. In the retail store, it's not healthy to internalize anger because you still believe it's wrong to complain about having been overcharged. As well is to simply fume over the overcooked steak at the restaurant and say nothing to the waiter. All you've done is replace the fear associated with speaking out with the anger of feeling wronged. Simply registering a complaint could so easily have dissipated that anger. I'll bet that if you really were to think about it, there are many things that you regret not having done out of fear. Even within the past 24 hours, you may well have stretched *turn the other cheek* beyond its intended boundary. Why? Probably because you wanted to avoid the fear that might have been precipitated had the other person responded like Dad did so many decades ago.

The first question to ask is, *"Is this belief that it's wrong to complain justified?"* The answer is *No*. There's nothing noble about being wronged and saying nothing. When you have been overcharged for a purchase, the belief that it is wrong to speak up is not justified.

"Is the belief serving a useful purpose?" Of course not. It's serving a harmful purpose. Doing nothing is one of the behaviors normally associated with a feeling of helplessness, a feeling that will erode your health faster than anything else.

Let's approach change by starting with the end. After all, it would require a great deal of time and the skills of a gifted therapist to travel back in time and revisit your early childhood to identify the cause of the belief. Instead, let's start at the end with the fear that you are trying to avoid. When you cast aside all the details, what you are left with is a belief that enables you to avoid the emotion of fear. That's what you can fix.

At my Saddlebrook Resort headquarters near Tampa, Florida, I have created a program that's designed to deal with what is probably the greatest impediment to personal growth and

99

corporate success: the fear of failure. I focus upon the issue of fear to start with and take people out of their comfort zone, away from all the things that provide security. They are taken into the woods where there are no walls displaying certificates of achievement; where there's no place for the coat and tie they rely upon to convey power and authority in the workplace; where the expensive gold watch or reserve of cash are of no value. That alone enables some people to push their personal comfort envelope and learn to deal with the mild fear of being in a novel environment. Of course, everyone is having fun during the process. They are playing games and enjoying themselves. There's no reason why learning a valuable lesson cannot also be fun. And, sometimes, this serves as a useful diversion, or what I refer to as emotional interference. The friendly exchanges, as people enter this unfamiliar territory, serve to counterbalance their uncertainty.

In this new environment, the old, familiar beliefs are easier to let go of as a new group with a different purpose and different dynamics begins to form, a group that now requires different skills to function effectively. This is the first critical step to change - getting rid of old, unhealthy beliefs. In this new environment, the ability to predict has vanished, giving rise to uncertainty. Our course includes ropes suspended from trees, wire bridges, a zip line, countless problem-solving initiatives, and a rock-climbing wall. Some people greet this new environment and the uncertainty it brings with excitement and even elation. Others clearly are uncomfortable being away from their normal routine. In his own way, each person is dealing with change on his own terms. I have created an environment where they can learn to overcome fear safely. The stock-boy with rock-climbing experience overcomes his nervousness of speaking to the owner of the company when it becomes clear to the group that his skills now are going to be a tremendous asset. And the CEO learns to deal with the discomfort of being in a subservient position and having little to offer in this new setting. No one is ever pressured into crossing out of his comfort zone. But, if they want to explore, one small step at a time, what it's like to experience a fear response and then recovery from it, they can do it safely, in a wonderfully supportive environment. That evening, they hear an after-dinner talk, using film clips of the day's activities, during which I discuss many of the issues I'm now delving into.

When it's over, people are better equipped to deal with the fears of change. They have learned to accept change and to cope with uncertainty on their terms so that when they experience similar challenges in the workplace or in their personal lives, they can do what my family does after an adventure vacation. The body can shrug off any new challenge by saying, *"Been there, done that, and got the tee-shirt, no problem."* Bring on the next challenge. It's Cross-Stressing.

It's just like a child acquiring a new language. Learning a foreign language is very difficult. But, once it's acquired, it becomes relatively easy to acquire another new language because the child now has a learning set for languages. What you can do is acquire a learning set for change. The ability to face the emotional consequences of change head-on will enable you to accept the risks you have to take to establish new boundaries in your professional and personal life.

If you cannot accept change, you will always remain where you are now in a world that is in a constant state of flux. This concept applies not just to the business world, but to your relationships, as well. A healthy business organization is a living system, constantly in the process of growing. Individuals who have the capacity to deal with change drive healthy companies. Healthy people also recognize that during the course of a relationship, they and their partner change. Healthy people are willing to constantly examine their beliefs as they prepare for inevitable change in both their personal and professional lives. But you cannot learn to change without accepting some

101

potential risk, if nothing else, the prospect of failure. The training itself can be risky as you face your beliefs head-on and set about to create new mental images to better match your ever-changing circumstances. Here's an exercise that I call *Pushing Your Emotional Envelope*.

Beginning today, I want you to practice dealing with change and the emotion of fear. For the next week, do one thing each day that is a departure from your normal way of behaving. It doesn't matter what it is. The only objective is to familiarize yourself with the feeling. And I'm not suggesting that you take up a dangerous sport or throw yourself in harm's way. There are many things that you can do that are quite safe from a physical standpoint, but which provide the opportunity to grow emotionally. Do you have a fear of public speaking? Then attend a PTA or city council meeting and make it a point to stand up and comment about an issue. Do the same at your next company training session. Ultimately, you might volunteer to make a presentation at a fundraiser or join a church choir. Is winning your objective? Even on the highway, where you always want to be in front of the car ahead? Or, first off the line at the traffic light? Then ease off on the accelerator, and be a follower. Let another motorist move ahead of you so that you can experience the emotion you have been trying to avoid. Are you always in control and the expert in your organization? Then become a volunteer. Spend some time at a homeless shelter, serving food or sweeping floors. Offer to help do something, knowing in advance that you have limited skills in this arena. Step out of your comfort zone, and learn to accept advice and instruction from others.

I once enrolled in a 5-day training program on how to run a ropes course. It was a new experience for me. For years, I'd been the person in front of the classroom, presenting the training and being asked the questions. Suddenly, I found myself immersed in a group of people half my age and with largely physical education backgrounds, instead of science. No one had any need for my information, and I had few answers to the questions being posed. Instead, I was doing the asking, while seeking the skills I eventually would need. I was a stranger in this environment. Even the frost during that fall in Massachusetts was a departure from the warmth I had grown accustomed to at my home in Florida. But, the experience gave me new insights about other aspects of my life. Just experiencing the feeling associated with that unfamiliar role provided me with a different way of looking at things.

There's another way you can teach yourself to better handle negative emotions – experience them on your terms and discover that they really aren't all that bad. When I conduct multi-day training programs, I will give participants an assignment to find a partner and do something that's legal and reasonably safe, but which takes them outside their emotional comfort zone. The reason I have them pair up is because there's safety in numbers, plus the other person provides the extra motivation that is sometimes needed. Here are some of the things people have done:

- Approach a stranger
- Swim in a public fountain
- Ride a roller coaster
- Gamble
- Hold a snake
- Go skinny dipping
- Eat unappealing food
- Sky dive
- Rock climb
- Argue with a friend
- Parasail
- Speak in public
- Wear outlandish clothes/makeup
- Bungee jump
- Climb a radio antenna
- Swim in cold water

- Jump off a high-diving platform
- Go to the top of a tall building
- Roller skate
- Confess a weakness to an admirer
- Say no when expected to say yes
- Ride on a motorcycle

Some of these things may be a part of your normal routine. However, for some individuals, these activities may offer an opportunity to experience what emotional discomfort can be like. More importantly, they got over it. That's the key element. Successfully recovering from adversity is how we learn to be optimistic. *"This, too, shall pass"* is the lesson learned. And if it's really bad, from that point on, you can reflect upon the experience, and when confronted with a different type of challenge, say to yourself, *"I'm glad I'm not* _____ (in cold water, bungee jumping, or whatever you did that raised your adrenalin).

Use successive approximation. Take small steps until you feel comfortable leaving your familiar surroundings and operating with a new set of beliefs. Examine each emotion that you experience along with your beliefs. By immersing yourself in novel environments, you'll develop the ability to accept and trust others, and to gain the confidence to accept change. Armed with those skills, there is no limit to what you will achieve.

You may totally agree with this advice, but still be reluctant. *I don't have time* or *It won't improve the appearance of my resume* may be the belief holding you back. I once was faced with that same dilemma. I'd been offered a very good job at the University of Texas Medical School in Galveston. It was a tenure-track position, which, even in those days, was difficult to secure. At the same time, I also was offered a position with the National Geographic Society to lead an expedition to study whales in the West Indies. I did all of the things you're supposed to do: I sought input from trusted academic advisors. One said, *"Nick, if you go down to the West Indies, you will be committing academic suicide. You'll never keep up; you'll forget everything you learned. Don't throw away your education."* And other people said the same thing. That's when I created two lists; one included all of the reasons why I should have accepted the job at the medical school in Texas, and I filled up a legal pad. And then I made a list of all of the reasons why I should go to the West Indies, and I could have fitted them onto a postage stamp.

But, I really wanted to go to the islands, so I re-framed the question. Instead of asking myself, *"What should I do?"* I asked, *"What will I regret not having done at some future date?"* And within weeks, my wife and I packed up our then six-month-old daughter and sailed off into the sunset. To this day, I have never had a real job, and, at this stage in my life, I probably never will. Did I make the right decision? I don't know. There's no way of ever knowing, so I don't even bother to ponder the matter. Do I have any regrets? Absolutely not. I've accumulated a treasure chest of experiences and, in the process, learned to adapt to just about every category of change. So, while you are thinking of reasons not to do the things you can and should, take a moment to step out of the present, and peer into the future. That new perspective may be just the vantage point that you need to make the right choice.

There's one more thing. You are converting one of the most powerful emotions you ever experience into a catalyst for change. Fear of regret is now replacing fear of failure. Instead of a fear holding you back, you now have converted it into a force to propel you forward.

BECAUSE I'LL ALWAYS BE THE WAY I AM

Who Are You And What Do You Want?

Who are you? When you introduce yourself to someone and have to give a one or two sentence explanation of who you are, how do you answer? Like this?

"Hi. I'm Nick Hall, Director of Important Stuff at the XYZ Corporation."

Is your identity attached to your work? If so, you might have too much of your self-esteem, of who you are as a person, tied to the workplace. If one day you awaken, and you are not Nick Hall, Director of Important Stuff at the XYZ Corporation, who would you be? What would you be if you lost your job tomorrow - and I'm not talking about the financial implications? If you lost your job tomorrow, how would you define yourself? You could no longer say, "I'm Director of Important Stuff." You could no longer say, "I work at the XYZ Corporation." Are you a daughter, a brother, a mother, a son? Are you a sailor, a gardener, a seamstress, a wood worker, an artist? Your personal identity will, in turn, shape your values, beliefs, and goals, which will impact on the progress you make toward a goal. If your beliefs are enabling you to make progress toward achieving your goals, I suspect the emotions you experience are largely positive and fulfilling. But, if your beliefs are keeping you from achieving your goals, you probably are experiencing many negative emotions. And, if you don't know what your beliefs or goals are, then you probably bounce from one emotional state to another without knowing why.

Why is it that some people live life so passionately and so fully? They work at jobs they love. They enjoy their family. They have mastered the art of pleasure, and they are rich in every aspect of their lives because they are living to their fullest potential. Could it be as simple as the fact that their system for living truly reflects their core beliefs and values? I think so.

Discovering What You Value

As I lecture around the country on beliefs, emotions, stress, and related mind/body issues, I find that most people don't really believe they can be whatever they want to be, or that they can do whatever it is they want to do. Their beliefs won't allow them to accept this. I find, too, that most people don't really value what they are currently doing, and they don't really value what they have or could have. And it's not for lack of trying. Do you know people who go to seminar after seminar? Who read self-help books and obediently complete audio programs, but they still can't seem to put it all together to make the necessary changes? Do you know someone like that? Even if they get a better job, they are still not happy. Oh, they might be happy for a little while, but the same problems seem to resurface at work and at home and with money. And then what happens? They get angry, afraid, depressed, or ashamed.

Their actions, the way they live, the jobs they work at, are not congruent with their core beliefs. And because their beliefs are in conflict with their lifestyle, it affects their emotional state in ways that are highly detrimental to their physical and mental health. It affects how they feel about themselves, the way they eat, whether or not they exercise, what they do for a living, the quality of their family life, and how they plan for the future.

So, how do you know who you are and what you really believe is important? Here's a fun way to find out what's near and dear to you. Imagine that you have just opened the door; standing there is a representative from a lottery with a check for 10 million dollars. But, there's a catch. You have 5 minutes to decide what to do with it – every last penny. And what you don't account for, you don't get. Start writing; and remember, you have only 5 minutes.

What immediately comes to mind? New house, new car, new clothes? Many people go directly to advertised beliefs, including what they believe success should look like, or, more likely, what they have been told being rich looks like. Be careful. You may be spending your money and redesigning your life based on somebody else's values. What about buying all those things for someone else? A mansion for your parents, a Mercedes for your best friend, a sport fishing boat for your brother-in-law, and two first class tickets on a cruise boat for a couple of friends?

What's up with the big spender? Just being a nice person? Look closer. It could very well be a hand-me-down belief. Maybe you think you don't deserve the money, and you need to give it away. Or you've heard that rich people aren't nice; they're miserly, and so you give it away instead of becoming like that. Or, maybe, as a child, you never had enough money, so you're going to spend everything you have to show people that you now have it. And then what happens is that you end up with nothing again.

Look at your lottery list. Is there a church or charitable organization mentioned? Or, did you immediately invest it all to make more money? What does this say about your values? Think carefully. Do you really need the purchases, or are you spending or not spending money in a way that is expected of you? What if you are unable to develop a list for all of this money? You have no idea what to do with it? Then you may not know what your core beliefs are, and you are going to have to dig a little deeper. Don't mistake the objective of this exercise. The intent is not to instill a particular belief – it's just to get you thinking about your own. There is no right or wrong belief. It's only when a belief is not justified for your circumstances or when it impedes your progress towards a worthwhile goal that it needs to be changed.

Here are some incomplete sentences. Take a break from reading, and finish the listed statement in a manner consistent with your beliefs and values.

Life is _____. A cynic might answer *a terminal disease.* A more positive response might be *a precious gift.*

The world would be a better place to live if _____. *There were no illnesses?* How about, *There were more goodwill.*

And here's one more example, which gets to the core of this process. *I am* _____.

Are you still uncertain about what it is you value? It goes hand in hand with your beliefs. Do you value money? power? labor? a higher power? Or, perhaps, family, your career, or material possessions? It matters less what you value. It does matter that you know what it is you value.

Create Your Blueprint

Here's another way to find out what you value. I'd like you to reflect for just a moment upon that one person in your life - a grandparent, parent, close friend, or, perhaps, a mentor - who always seems to make the right decision, no matter how much pressure that person is under. Someone whose behavior you have tried to emulate when you've found yourself under difficult circumstances. How would you describe this person? What words come to mind that characterize this person to whom you look up? Chances are this person reflects your own beliefs and values. Or, at least what you would like them to be. Most often, when I ask that question of audiences, I hear words like: *balanced, controlled, confident, compassionate, caring, flexible, energized, calm, and peaceful.*

Do those sound like the words on your list? If these are the common characteristics of people you admire, then they are probably the characteristics that you most value and desire to have yourself. You can become that person. And the first important step is experiencing that realization of what you want to be. Let's look closely at that list again.

Balanced. These are people who don't just talk the talk; they walk the walk. They have a good balance of work and family time. They eat well and exercise. They relax and play. They are involved in their communities. They have plenty of social interaction, yet they take the time to reflect and allow time for themselves. They live a balanced life. Most importantly, they conduct their lives in a manner that is consistent with their beliefs and value system. They don't deviate. Their value system is like an old friend, a constant that keeps them centered, even during the most severe stress.

Controlled. These are people who are in control. But, by control, I do not mean the ability to manipulate or to control other people. Instead, they are in control of their own emotions, and, as a result of not allowing anger, fear, or sadness interfere with their objectives, they are able to remain focused. A values-driven belief provides a foundation for their lives.

Confident. They are people who are able to do things with seemingly very little effort and, as a consequence, they are, indeed, confident. In addition, they are able to instill confidence in others, which is why people often gravitate towards them.

Compassionate and Caring. They are individuals who often engage in altruistic pursuits. They believe in the inherent good of all people. They do not prejudge others.

111

Flexible and Energized. These are people who are active physically as well as mentally. They are open-minded people who gather as much information as they can so that their perception of the world is realistic.

Calm and Peaceful. They have core beliefs that match their system of living. Their way of life reflects what they believe. They are in their optimal emotional state - that condition when the emotion they feel and express will help propel them towards a worthwhile goal. They are healthy, working and living to their fullest potential. They also have maximum functional capacity right up until the end.

What prevents you from accessing this optimal emotional state? First, think of the times you have been able to access this state. Everything seems to flow easily; your thinking is clearer, you perform better, and you accomplish more; you are relaxed, and you feel good about yourself and what you are doing. Maybe it happened once on the golf course – one of those days where you just couldn't miss. Or the time you gave a presentation and pulled it off flawlessly. Or, wrote a paper effortlessly. Or, put together that new intergalactic spacecraft with your six-year-old. You hardly needed directions. Remember those times when you weren't anxious or frustrated. You were balanced, controlled, confident, compassionate, caring, flexible, energized, calm, and peaceful.

What stops you from accessing this state more often? What prevents you from acquiring those qualities you most admire in your favorite person? An erroneous belief? Here are some of the most common I've heard, which, invariably, are not justified and impede progress towards a goal.

- I'm awkward in crowds.
- I never do well on exams.
- There's nothing I can do about it.

112

- It runs in my family.
- Failure is bad; I must always succeed.
- Stress is bad, and it should be avoided.
- I'm too old to change.
- I'm no good at relationships.
- Nice guys finish last.

Any of these sound familiar? Then accept the Belief Challenge, and, if warranted, change your belief.

Some beliefs may be very difficult to change – especially when they are cultural, as many are. Look at your workplace culture. Do you believe you have to work a tremendous amount of over- time to get ahead? Do you believe that if you tell colleagues you are taking off early to see your daughter in a play or to go out with your husband to celebrate your wedding anniversary, they won't take you seriously? I know workplaces where it's considered a badge of courage not to take a vacation. People are proud of having stored up 100 or more vacation days. Some people display million mile tags on their airline baggage. To me, it says the time they spend on their work is out of proportion with time spent with family, with community, and with self. And I know they are not nearly as productive as they think they are. They are driven by some of the common beliefs of their culture, instead of their own value system. For just a moment, project your mind in space and time to the future. I know this is a bit morbid, but when you are lying on your deathbed, in your hour of final reflection, do you think that you're going to wish that you'd spent more time at the office, or more time with your family?

Let's now consider advertised beliefs and the concept of balance. Picture this. There's a guy with his family in front of a sculpture at the Whitney Museum, and he takes out his cell phone to check in with work. Cut to a new scene: there's a woman having lunch with her mother at a lovely restaurant, but she has her notebook computer on the table, checking her e-mail. Almost all advertisements surrounding technology want you to believe that you can have more downtime because you can be connected with work while you relax. This is a contradiction. You need to unplug, unwind, and just relax when you relax. Enjoy nothing else but the art in the museum when you are there, sharing the experience with your family. And don't miss out on the great conversation over lunch with your mom. Be where you are. That's an important part of living a centered life. When your life is in balance, your access to the optimal emotional state is easy and effortless.

Where Are You Going?

Now that you have identified your beliefs and your value system, what do you want to do with them? What do you want out of life? Many people live their entire life without ever asking this question, and, as a consequence, they fail to extract from life all that they might have had. A childhood prayer concludes: *...if I should die before I wake, I pray the Lord my soul to take*. A sad thought. Just as sad would be the substitution of the words: *...if I should die before I live*. Too many people drift aimlessly through life without a clear understanding of what they truly want. They eventually die at a ripe, old age, but they die before they have lived. More than likely, they never had any meaningful goals. Don't let this happen to you. Identify your personal goals now. Complete these statements, and do so on a regular basis, so that you don't forget.

In my lifetime, I want to _____.

Prior to retirement, I want to _____

Before my children have left home, I want to _____.

By _____, I want to _____.

114

Now ask yourself these questions:

- Are these goals attainable?
- Are they my goals or those of someone else?
- Are they stated concisely and as a positive objective?
- Am I willing to begin now? If not, under what circumstances will I begin?
- Am I willing to make changes in my life to achieve my goals?
- Are my goals consistent with my values and beliefs?
- Do any of my goals conflict with each other?
- What am I willing to give up to achieve my goals?

Establishing unrealistic goals is a sure way to doom you to failure. It's important to set goals for yourself. It's your life. Do what feels right for you, not what you think is expected of you by associates or by family members. You also must make a commitment to achieve your goals. Many people get involved in various projects that they believe will help them reach their objective, but they fail to get there because they don't make a commitment. True commitment means making sacrifices and delaying gratification. Establishing unrealistic goals is an effort in futility. And identifying goals that are inconsistent with your values and beliefs will be a constant source of conflict.

Ten Beliefs That Can Block Your Progress

There are some beliefs based upon biases or faulty perceptions that interfere with growth and personal happiness, regardless of the environment. Often these beliefs are learned during childhood and are reinforced throughout life. We know intellectually that these perspectives are faulty, but we have difficulty changing due to the strong emotions associated with the belief. Often these beliefs are so ingrained that we use them without thinking, despite the fact that they can lead to feelings of sadness, hopelessness, fear, or anxiety. The following are ten common beliefs with which many people

115

struggle. As you review them, ask yourself which of these 10 beliefs operate consciously or unconsciously in your life.

1. *I must be loved, validated, and approved by everyone.* This belief keeps you from being yourself for fear that you will meet with disapproval or rejection. Individuals who subscribe to this belief often cheat themselves out of being who they are, focusing instead on evaluating situations and other people for how to respond. As a result, difficulties in both professional and personal relationships are common due to the fact that a healthy relationship requires two separate individuals who respect their own and each other's identity.

2. *I am responsible for other people.* By taking responsibility for others, you may inadvertently take away their motivation to accept responsibility for themselves. In addition, you put yourself in a no-win situation. Controlling other people is rarely, if ever, possible. When you do this, you lose touch with yourself. How do people get this way? They often come from families where everyone made unreasonable demands or were possessive of others. They have little respect for another person's individual identity because they never learned what it means. Instead of being open and soliciting dialogue, they attempt to read other people's minds and probe into their affairs, believing they have every right to do so. They can't see the boundary between where their self ends and another's begins. They have a very precarious sense of their own identity.

3. *My happiness depends on people and on things outside of myself.* Many people try to achieve inner happiness through other people or other things. While other people or things may provide you with some temporary comfort or pleasure, they cannot provide lasting happiness. Ultimately, your happiness depends on you. It's not

that simple, though. You need to be flexible and to adapt to the circumstances. Basically, when things are going well, you want to have a strong sense of being involved and of being a part of the process. This is something that psychologists refer to as an internal locus of control. But when things are going badly, you need to step out of that role. Give it your best shot, but recognize that there are some things that you simply cannot control, such as another person's behavior. Now, a sense of external locus of control can be beneficial. A healthy response is being able to say, "*I did all that I could, but, ultimately, the decision was made by someone I couldn't influence.*" When you don't even try, it may be because you attribute whatever happens in your life to outside factors.

4. *I must be the best at everything I do -- I can't make mistakes.* Perfectionism is a battle that many people fight every day. It is important to accept that everybody has areas of strength and weakness -- to be human is to be imperfect. While everybody likes to excel, no one can possibly excel at everything. Most successful people have succeeded only after many failures or mistakes. Life is a learning experience. Some people cannot acknowledge an imperfection because they never received the love and support to feel comfortable with their shortcomings. Deep down, they feel like worthless human beings, and they end up making unreasonable demands upon themselves and, sometimes, on others. In that unrealistic, over demanding world, they are able to justify their belief that they are hopeless because their self-imposed demands are so unrealistic. In order to feel good about themselves, they will project their faults onto other individuals or groups and blame them for whatever goes wrong. In short, when they criticize others, they are really revealing their own shortcomings.

117

"She rises at 6:00am, meditates for half an hour, wakes up her 2.3 kids, feeds them a grade A nutritious breakfast (which they eat), sends them off to school, puts on a $600 Anne Klein suit, goes to her $125,000 job, which is creative and socially useful, runs six miles on her lunch break, spends a wonderful hour of genuine, quality time with her children after school, then cooks a gourmet meal in her spotless designer kitchen. While cooking dinner, she discusses economic trends with her husband, and then, during family mealtime, continues to relate to her husband and children about meaningful topics. After the children are tucked in bed, she spends more quality time with her husband, and ends the evening with several hours of passionate lovemaking with multiple orgasms. She then has a good night's sleep, and in the morning she wakes refreshed and eager to start all over again."

Obviously, if you believe each day should resemble this description of Superwoman penned by the newspaper columnist, Ellen Goodman, you are going to have very low self-esteem as you constantly fail to achieve this unrealistic standard. By the way, perfectionism is okay in some environments. It's good that engineers at NASA are perfectionists. And you want your surgeon to adhere to the highest standards imaginable.

5. *I can avoid dealing with problems or pain in life.* While you can postpone addressing difficulties and pain in life, you cannot completely avoid tough times indefinitely. Accepting them and dealing with problems and emotions directly allows you to put them behind you. Avoiding emotions is rarely effective for the long term. It is not possible to fully enjoy positive feelings when you have denied negative feelings. It is the failure to acknowledge an emotion that will wreak havoc in your life. I'm not suggesting that you walk into your boss' office and engage in a form of emotional exhibitionism. Carefully chose the right time and place. Remember,

the emotion is signaling a perceived unmet need or problem that needs to be addressed. Denying the emotion is ignoring the problem. You have a choice. You can deal with it consciously on your terms, or you can wait for it to surprise you when your body can't take it anymore.

6. *Inconveniences in life are catastrophes.* It is important to keep the daily hassles and inconveniences in life in proper perspective. What is the worst-case scenario? Is it really as bad as you fear? Life is full of problems. Your choice is whether or not you accept this fact or repeatedly set yourself up for disappointment by expecting life to be hassle-free. Paradoxically, when you accept this fact, the hassles become easier to tolerate.

7. *I must be in control at all times.* It is a fact that there are many things in life beyond our control. However, we are consistently in control of our attitude, or our happiness. If we believe in the illusion of control, we will repeatedly face the impossible task of trying to govern what is beyond us. While it is beneficial to maintain control over situations that we can influence, the belief that we have power over all events is an illusion that is responsible for much unhappiness. As I noted previously, it's good to have control over some things. But problems arise when control becomes the end instead of the means, when we refuse to relinquish it even when circumstances call for delegation or simply letting go. Reinhold Niebuhr said it best: "*God, grant me the serenity to accept the things I cannot change, courage to change the things I can, and wisdom to know the difference.*"

8. *If people knew the real me, they would not like me.* This belief can cause you to pretend to be someone you are not, ultimately distancing yourself from other people,

including those people who might truly appreciate and enjoy the person you really are. The bad news is that you probably do have some traits or features that others might consider undesirable. The good news is that everyone does. Furthermore, when you can see your own limitations, it becomes easier to accept those of others. You'll be more realistic and not expect people to be more wonderful than they really are. There will be other benefits as well. You'll have less of a tendency to exaggerate the negative.

9. *It is wrong to enjoy myself too much.* While life is sometimes painful and difficult, it is healthy to enjoy life and to make a decision to seek fulfillment and joy out of the experiences available to you. Once you accept this, you become closer to and appreciate more the people around you.

10. *I can't change because I've always been the way that I am.* If you truly believe this, it is unlikely that you will change because you have sealed yourself off. Choices are made each and every moment in life. While making changes is sometimes very difficult, you effect change simply by making choices. What characterizes truly healthy people is having the capacity to deal with change. Often, they thrive on it as they view events not as obstacles but as challenges. Many people can't seem to maintain openness and flexibility, and they end up distraught when things don't turn out as they expected. For these people, even minor changes can make them feel overwhelmed.

These ten beliefs often interfere with your professional development and personal enrichment. They will keep you from achieving your goals by giving rise to unhealthy emotions and inappropriate responses.

BECAUSE IT WON'T MAKE ANY DIFFERENCE

Take Control Over Your Life

By posing questions and examining your beliefs, you have begun to take control. No, not control over other people, but control over yourself. Many people believe they have no choice but to relinquish control to others, especially under duress. They become embroiled in an altercation with their supervisor and then adopt the attitude that, *"There's nothing I can do. If I say anything or do anything, it won't make any difference, and I'll probably lose my job."* They believe they are helpless. This can wreak havoc upon the body. A very important belief to have is that you can do something. I'll briefly review three studies to illustrate just what I mean.

First, experiments have revealed that when rats are stressed, if they are able to press a bar and turn the stressor off, this control will offset some of the health problems that would arise if they lacked this control. In short, it is not the stressor that causes the health problems, but the belief that they have no control over it.

Second, if rats have had control, and then the bar is disconnected, they still do better than rats that never had any control. This is because they believe things are still better. They still get shocked after pressing the bar, but based upon the previous experience, they perceive things are not as bad.

Third, a large group of rats was given 10 shocks an hour. The day before, half of the rats received 20 shocks, and half received just one. Who suffered the most, even though the stressor is now identical for both groups? It was the group that previously received just one shock. Why? Because going from

20 shocks to 10 instills a sense of optimism that things are getting better, while those animals that went from 1 shock to 10 have nothing to be optimistic about; for them, things are getting worse.

These, and many other, well-controlled studies, clearly reveal that the belief that we are in control, even in the absence of any benefit, coupled with the belief that things are improving, are sufficient to not only lessen the stress response, but, significantly, to reduce the probability of developing stress-related illnesses. However, be careful with this concept of control. Too much control can be just as detrimental to your health as too little. This was revealed through studies in Vietnam. Investigators found that it was middle management, or the middle-level officers, who had to make a lot of very important decisions affecting the lives of many men under their command, who suffered most from the effects of stress, as compared to those troops who simply followed orders and went out into the rice paddies. So, having too much control – or too much responsibility –also can be detrimental to your health.

But, being completely helpless is also a serious problem. That is why I strongly recommend that you always do something in a stress situation, even if the probability of a positive outcome is very remote. What is important is that you not act like a victim. So often when a person is in the midst of an altercation, especially in the workplace, they will shrug their shoulders, walk away from the problem, and adopt the attitude that, *"There is nothing I can do. If I say anything or do anything, I will probably be put on the night shift for the rest of my life."* Or, *"I'll never get another day off. I might even lose my job."* So they walk down to the coffee pot, and they talk about the person behind his back, which, by the way, I strongly recommend you do. It's when you internalize an emotion that it wreaks havoc on your immune system and on your overall health. If that's all you do, it is going to be extremely detrimental to your health. When you walk away with the attitude that there is nothing you can do, you are acting like a victim, thereby, making your belief a self-fulfilling prophecy. If all you do is talk about the person, you will fuel your emotion without addressing the problem that gave rise to it. Ultimately, it will be detrimental not only to the person you are talking about, but to yourself as well.

While it's okay to talk about the situation, it's preferable to do it with the person who has triggered your response. It may turn out that doing nothing is the best thing to do. But if you do nothing, make sure it is because you choose this as one of several options. Don't do *nothing* because you believe that your hands are tied and that there are no other choices. Sometimes, doing nothing is, indeed, the best choice to make. But make sure that you give yourself a metaphorical bar to press.

However, it is not always this simple. The fact is *one size does not fit all.* There are some people who believe that they must have complete control and responsibility over as many things in their environment as possible. And then there are other people who believe that it is best for someone else to do it all. There is nothing wrong with either belief. Problems arise when people who want responsibility and control are in situations where this desired responsibility and control are not available. Or, when people who feel more comfortable having someone else make the decisions are suddenly put in the driver's seat. Once again, the problem is a mismatch between people's beliefs and their environment.

Additional conflict may arise because people change. You are not the same person under stress that you are when all is calm. Under pressure, you may become just the opposite of what you usually are. Most of the time, people will adhere to the belief that they developed in their family unit, so if they were encouraged to be inquisitive, or to argue, that's probably the way they'll be the rest of their lives. If they were encouraged to be silent and not to speak up, that will be their tendency. Then people will seek out employment and environments where there is a match between the ways they are comfortable responding and what they have to do. Under stress, however, the rules change. The same people who want control in times of calm may become acquiescing or accommodating under stress. On the other hand, people who have been accommodators will now suddenly seize the reins of control. But because this type of response is not one they are accustomed to experiencing, this lack of familiarity may give rise to yet another source of conflict. Realize that the critical variable of control is not a simple one.

Actually, I'm not even sure if *control* itself should be the objective. Instead, it needs to be viewed as a process for achieving closure. Of course, you are more likely to experience closure when you are in control. At the same time, I think it is all right for someone else to have that control as long as the person giving it up is comfortable with the arrangement. There are some people who, obviously, cannot completely control their medical circumstances, but they trust in their doctor or other healthcare provider. The belief that the doctor is in control and will make the right decision can be just as good in accomplishing closure. So can a belief in a higher power -- believing that what is happening to me right now is part of some large, unified plan -- and that there is, ultimately, going to be a beneficial outcome. You don't have to know what that outcome will be, or what direction things are going to go. But whether they get worse or whether they get better, the belief that this is part of some large plan and that there will, eventually, be closure can help some people deal with turmoil.

When All Else Fails

Sometimes you simply can't control things. The environment might have failed so rapidly that there's not a darn thing you can do about it. And you may have very limited control over your physical or behavioral responses. You may be paralyzed - perhaps with fear. But there is always one thing you do have control over right up until your dying breath, and that is your attitude, which no one can take away from you. You cannot really control another person's behavior, nor can they control what you do. Granted, it may be extremely difficult to control your responses to another person's actions. But, ultimately, that control resides within you via your attitude, and it just may save your life.

I have a very good friend whose life was saved because of his attitude. He just retired as a special agent in charge of a tactical training program at the FBI Academy. We now work together creating adventure programs at Saddlebrook Resort for corporate clients who want to learn how to overcome fear. In the late 1960's, Phil was in Vietnam as part of a special unit that was ambushed by the enemy. Everyone in the unit was killed, except Phil, who should have died. He was hit 13 times with bullets from AK47 machine guns. But, he survived against all medical odds. I once asked him why? Why it was he was able to overcome such medical odds. He replied, *"While I was lying on the ground unable to move, feeling the life literally drain out of me, I was absolutely determined that I was going to stay awake so when the enemy came over to slit my throat or put a bullet in my head, I was going to spit in their faces and glare at them so that they would know that I was dying on my terms and not on theirs."* Well, it turned out that he had killed the enemy. There was no one left to slit his throat, so he remained awake until, eventually, an evacuation helicopter arrived.

That is exactly the type of fighting spirit that Dr. Bernie Segal writes and lectures about, a spirit that characterizes individuals who do not accept the belief of others. When they are told by their healthcare provider that the odds of surviving the cancer are very remote, they reply by saying, *"My body doesn't know about statistics. I am not average. I'm going to be the exception."* They are the people who take control. They fight until the bitter end, and often they overcome seemingly insurmountable odds, just as Victor Frankel did when he was incarcerated in the Nazi concentration camps. He was once asked why it was he survived when so many others died from starvation, disease, and torture. His answer was eloquent in its simplicity, *"The belief that one day I would be asked that question."* He was able to see beyond the barbed wire, as he remained optimistic that there would be life after the camp. In addition, he seized control over those things in his life that he could influence. There was much he wasn't able to control; but, by ritualizing the act of brushing his teeth in the morning and by making a big production of getting dressed, he seized control over the small things in his environment that he was able to influence. He never surrendered his spirit to that feeling of total helplessness.

No one sprinkles you with magical dust to induce a belief that you can't do something. No one presses a button in the side of your head that induces an emotion. These are your responses, and no one can ever control them for you. No one. In the end, the very belief, 'You are in control,' may save your life. It may also enable you to endure one of the greatest fears we have in Western society, which is the fear of dying.

Several years ago, I learned of a study that is currently illegal in the state in which it was carried out. Some would consider it to be immoral, as well, although I'll leave that judgment up to you, the reader. It involved assisted suicide, and it went on for a number of years. Despite what you read in newspapers, Dr. Kevorkian, probably, is the rule, not the exception. But, most doctors involved do not make a political issue out of it. I was giving a lecture on spirituality and healing at a national gathering of clergy. All of the major religions and denominations were represented. There were rabbis, priests, and ministers. The one thing that they shared in common was specializing in ministering to people who were dying. Many of them were hospital chaplains or worked for Hospice. Of course, I was surprised that members of the cloth would be doing this type of research because it seemed counter to their religious teachings. When I raised this issue, their overwhelming reply was that if a person is ever in need of their spiritual resources, it is when they are making that final transition from life to death. They were going to be there for that person.

In this study, when a patient asked for an extract of hemlock or for a medication that would enable them to terminate the dying process, the doctor would make it available, but not administer it. *"Here it is. I'm going to leave it on this table or place it in this drawer within easy reach. And this is how much you take."* Then the member of the clergy granted the person permission by telling them that it was okay. I was informed that out of more than two dozen people, not a single one chose to take that final step, even though all initially had requested the lethal medication dose to be administered. Of course, this resolves both the legal and moral dilemma because it was no longer assisted suicide. It turned out that they weren't afraid of being dead – what they were afraid of was the process of dying. *"Will I lose control?"-- "Will I be in excruciating pain?"* -- *"Will I be a burden to my loved ones?"* They were provided with the means by which they could believe they were in control. Simply the perception or the image of having control, right up until their dying breath, was all that it took to enable them to deal with the issue. If being in control overcomes the fear of dying, can you imagine what benefits it could provide in lesser circumstances? Never give up.

Personality and Goals

I'm sure that you've heard of the so-called Type A personality, the person who is always in a hurry, who never takes time out to smell the roses, who often speaks rapidly, and who finishes your sentences for you because he gets impatient waiting for you to finish saying whatever it is you're going to say, probably because whatever you have to say is not important to him in the first place.

There is a certain amount of overlap between the Type A personality and what is referred to as the *controlling personality*. This person is basically in a win/lose mode. *"I'm going to win; you're going to lose. We are going to do it my way, or we are not going to do it at all."* This person is personally threatened by dialogue. If you disagree with him, he'll take it as a personal affront. *"Why waste time talking about the problem? We're going to do it my way, anyway, so let's just get on with it."*

You've probably heard that it is the time-oriented, controlling personality who is most likely to succumb to a heart attack. Well, that's only partially correct. That was the interpretation of the data from the Framingham Heart Study when first completed. And on the basis of the limited information available to the psychologists at that time, that was the correct interpretation. But, it was only a correlation. Subsequently, Dr. Redford Williams and others designed more expansive studies. It turns out that they discovered there was something else that accounted for most of the correlations between the Type A personality and coronary arterial disease. Anger and hostility, the emotions of stress, were largely responsible. In other words, it's all right to be a workaholic, just don't be an angry, hostile workaholic. And if you are, for heaven's sake, don't internalize it. That makes things even worse.

Let's consider now the so-called Type C personality. This is the person who is the opposite of the controller, one you would call the accommodator. This person is in a lose/win mode. *"I'm going to lose; you're going to win. Your needs are more important than mine. There's no point in talking about this since we're going to do it your way, anyway."* This is the person Lydia Temoshok labeled as the Type C or cancer-prone personality. This is the person George Solomon described as being susceptible to rheumatoid arthritis. This is a very passive individual, one who will experience a great deal of personal discomfort in order to please other people. Evidence suggests that they have a difficult time dealing with negative emotions, especially in others. In a clinical setting, this person will wait until his throat is parched before troubling the staff for a glass of water. Then he will apologize for having taken your time. He is just the opposite of that Type A on the second floor, the one who constantly is demanding the nurses' time, wanting to know, *"Why am I taking this pill and that pill, and what do you mean waking me at 2 o'clock in the morning to give me a sleeping pill?"* He is the person who in the clinical setting is often labeled as difficult to manage. It's no surprise that's the person who does not get much voluntary attention. Yet, despite this, the demanding person is the one who is most likely going to survive, whereas the passive, sweet individual is likely to experience a worse outcome.

Reflect for just a moment on these two personalities, but from the standpoint of control. The person asking the questions would not do so if he did not believe that there were going to be an outcome. In other words, he has made himself a part of the negotiation of his treatment. He has given himself a metaphorical bar to press. In contrast, the Type C individual has basically abdicated responsibility, handing it over to the healthcare provider. *"Here I am. Do whatever you will."* Oh, I'm sure that there are many factors and explanations as to why one person has a better prognosis than another. But, in view of the data that I briefly summarized a little while ago, there is no question in my mind that giving up control is a very important variable. Acting like a victim is never healthy.

There's another personality type that you hear about, which is the so-called Type T or Thrill Seeking personality. These are people who take calculated risks and include bungee jumpers, skydivers, and motorcycle racers. It is the Type T individual who does not accept conventional wisdom or certain existing

129

beliefs. This is a person who explores new horizons and who is always looking for a different way to do things. This is the person who makes discoveries and who is not afraid of risk, indeed, who thrives on it. It doesn't hurt to have at least a small amount of Type-T in your makeup. After all, doing something different, even if it's positive, carries the inherent risk of failure. An unwillingness to take such risks may be what's holding you back.

There are other personalities as well. For example, there's the collaborator, who is in a win/win mode. *"I want to win, but I'm concerned about your needs. I want you to win as well."* This person is very different from the controller. Collaborators are energized by disagreement. They welcome dialogue.

There are also avoiders, who are the corporate equivalent of repressors. *"Problem? What problem?"* These same people fail to acknowledge unmet needs within their own body, just as they neglect important issues in the workplace.

These are just a few of the designations used to describe personality types. I want you to realize that there is nothing wrong with any of them. Just like beliefs, it is not the personality that is good or bad, but the context in which it is exhibited. Thank goodness all of our mothers were, at least temporarily, Type C's. Thank goodness they were willing to sacrifice their own need for sleep in order to nurture us as infants. We would never have survived if they had not been willing to do that. In that environment, being a Type C is a beneficial response. It is not good, however, when you are recovering in a hospital bed, and you place other people's needs ahead of your own – not when you are the one who needs the nurturing.

You might believe the collaborator is the best way to be, and it, most certainly, is in many environments, especially the business environment. When I'm lecturing to corporate clients, that is exactly what I encourage them to be like. The focus used to be on always winning. Now, a more collaborative stance is advocated for many work environments. Organizations recognize that even their competitors play a useful role in the economic eco-system.

But there are times when being the collaborator is not the best way to be. If you happen to be a law enforcement agent staring down a criminal's gun, that is not the time to be asking, *"Look, I really want to know what your needs are. How about I just cuff one of your hands, would that be all right?"* In law enforcement, coming in second is not good enough. Winning is everything, just as it is in the healthcare setting. When you are the person who has been diagnosed with cancer, you don't want your doctor coming up to you and saying, *"Look, there is a treatment for which you are an ideal candidate, and it's practically guaranteed to put your cancer into remission. The problem is it is still considered by some insurance companies, including yours, as being experimental, so they won't pay for it. But that's okay. There's another treatment. It's not as good, although there's still an 80 percent chance you'll survive by using that treatment."* You are not going to accept that kind of collaboration. There is only one option in that circumstance, and that is the best and the most effective treatment. If the insurance doesn't cover it, you expect the doctor to be your advocate and figure out a way to get you into that experimental protocol.

For everything, there is a season. That includes your personality – or, rather, your personalities. You see, we are really each composites of these different personalities. I hope you don't interact with your children in the same way that you interact with your coworkers. I hope you don't treat your spouse in the way that you treat subordinates at work. I hope your personality does vary depending upon the circumstance. And for that reason, I wish we could dispense with the label 'personality' altogether because it's really a coping style. Problems arise when the coping style or personality displayed is inappropriate for the environment. And when does that happen? When your beliefs give rise to mental images that fail to accurately depict reality. As Alfred Korzybski, the noted semanticist states, "The map is not the territory." If you want to do the things you know you can, but you just don't, realize that you need a healthy mix of several personalities.

BECAUSE I'M TOO SICK

The immune system doesn't get much media attention, but it should because it plays such an important role in your life. You may know what to do, but if your immune system is not working properly, it will be exceedingly difficult to remain focused and motivated. The immune system provides the body with a defense against invading microorganisms. Like any army, it needs to be fed, exercised, and kept sharp. When called into action, it attacks viruses by launching cellular cruise missiles that seek out intruders and destroy them. This first-strike ability not only keeps invaders at bay, but it also keeps important functions like memory and the ability to react in a ready state.

Your Body's Defense System

While not usually considered a part of the classic immune system, the skin is, nonetheless, an integral part. It is more than a protective barrier, preventing microbes from entering the body. While it does function in this manner, it is important to recognize that fatty acids, along with the secretions of sebaceous glands, can exert antimicrobial activity. Also present in the skin are bacterial flora, which not only are harmless, but, by competing with potentially dangerous bacteria, play a protective role. This role is enhanced through the production of natural antibiotics. Why would bacteria produce something capable of hastening their destruction? Because bacteria, if not regulated, will eventually die in their own waste.

Equally important lines of defense are mucous secretions. Most pathogens do not enter through the skin. Instead, they are inhaled or placed into the oral cavity on the backs of forks, toothbrushes, or hands. In order to block disease, an elaborately protective system has evolved. It includes saliva, which contains enzymes capable of breaking down not only food but also microbial organisms. In addition, saliva contains an antibody called secretory IgA. Found in all secretions, IgA can survive the harsh environment of the oral cavity due to the presence of a protein called the J-chain. IgA sticks to microbes, preventing them from advancing. Pro-inflammatory cytokines also are present in saliva. Inflammation, while troublesome when occurring in a confined space such as joints, is actually the first step in ridding the body of harmful pathogens. Saliva contains IL-1, which is an important molecule in this process.

Most people can remember what happened the first time they had to speak in public. It was probably in school when they were asked to make a short presentation. That's when speaking became next to impossible due to the inhibition of salivation. During stress, stored energy is broken down into its component parts. Anabolic or building processes are put on hold. Since digestion is technically a *building* process, it is one of the first to be impacted by stress. Salivation is part of the digestive system, so inhibition of this first step is a common consequence of the stress response. Of course, with less saliva, there will be less IgA, IL-1, as well as the enzymes capable of breaking down microbes. It is not surprising, then, that many people experience more infections associated with the oral cavity during times of duress. This was put to a direct, experimental test by scientists at Ohio State University, who found that wound healing within the oral cavity is delayed by emotional upheaval.

Secretions within the nasal passages play a similar, preventative role. Not only do microbes become trapped within the secretions and hair cells, but IgA facilitates their removal. This is why breathing through the nose can help prevent illness. This also explains why marathon runners are more susceptible to upper respiratory infections.

134

It is extremely difficult to remain properly hydrated when running non-stop for hours on end. Consequently, the athlete will produce less saliva and mucous secretions within the nasal passages. In addition, the final, competitive burst may well be accompanied with breathing through the mouth, which will enable pathogens to bypass the normal filtering systems and to enter the lungs directly. Other factors, including sustained production of glucocorticoids, are thought to contribute to this type of athlete's increased susceptibility to infection as well. In conclusion, these defense systems are extremely important; and when they are compromised, health consequences will ensue.

Additional enzymes and bacteriocins are present in the gut, which is the site of entry for food-borne pathogens. It also is a primary portal in infants. One of the numerous health benefits associated with breast-feeding is the IgA found in the colostrum of a mother's milk. Copious amounts of this antibody protect the infant against microbes.

In addition to these defenses, there are additional processes that play a crucial role in synergizing with the immune system. One is the fever response, and the other is sleep. Many people subscribe to the mistaken belief that fever is a symptom. While it certainly can be dangerous if excessive, fever also is an important part of the process whereby disease-causing organisms are combated. Many bacteria cannot survive if temperature goes up even a small amount. If they do survive, there is evidence that the immune system operates more efficiently against a backdrop of elevated temperature. Indeed, it is important enough to be coordinated by the immune system. IL-1 plays multiple roles in host defense. This macrophage-derived cytokine helps to mobilize T-lymphocytes; it is a pro-inflammatory agent and is the body's natural pyrogen. Other cytokines produced by cells of the immune system include IL-6, tumor necrosis factor alpha, and interferon alpha.

Sleep is another process essential for bringing about a state of optimal immunity. Each stage of sleep is distinct and correlated with specific events. A combination of stages 3 and 4 (otherwise known as slow-wave or delta) represent the interval during which large amounts of growth hormone are released. This release is especially pronounced during the first episode of slow-wave sleep during a given cycle. As its name implies, growth hormone stimulates the growth of cells. During an immune response, such growth would be manifested as the proliferation of an expanded population of T and B cells with specificity for the inciting microbe. IL-1 stimulates slow-wave sleep, thereby, triggering the release of this growth-promoting hormone at precisely the time it is needed by lymphocytes.

It's noteworthy that during exercise, IL-1 is released by muscle, ostensibly to stimulate via growth hormone its growth and repair. However, those same molecules of growth hormone also will assist the mobilization of lymphocytes, which may explain why people who exercise are healthier than those who are sedentary. Therefore, anything that interferes with the quality of sleep is going to impact on the immune system. Insomnia is a common symptom of stress, and some coping strategies, such as alcohol consumption, interfere directly with the slow-wave stage.

Chronic Fatigue and The Immune System

It is not surprising, given the close association between sleep and immunity, that disorders of one system might be related to the other. While the evidence is far from being conclusive, there is reason to believe that some forms of chronic fatigue may involve a perturbed state of immunity, possibly in association with stress.

Chronic Fatigue Syndrome is, by definition, a collection of symptoms. The causes of the same cluster of symptoms may vary from one individual to another, complicating not only the diagnosis of this elusive condition but also arriving at a viable treatment. It may well be that in some individuals, fatigue may be the culmination of chronic stress with immune system involvement. In addition to fatigue, some of the behavioral consequences of excessive immunity include symptoms of depression. It could be argued that engaging in withdrawal behaviors while the immune system is engaged in combating an infection would protect the organism. First, energy substrates could be diverted to the immune system, instead of being utilized in non-essential pursuits. Second, there could be additional risks when emotion-numbing cytokines are present. Staying out of a potentially hostile environment would be conducive to survival. Problems would arise if these basic mechanisms were activated at a time when the immune system was not required to combat an infection. For example, the microbe is under control, but the immune system continues to be stimulated. This is thought to be the cause of some forms of Chronic Fatigue Syndrome. In addition, many of the cytokines produced by an activated immune system are directly responsible for the symptoms that result in our feeling miserable when burdened with the flu or a bad cold. The intent is to keep us emotionally flat, so that we won't feel motivated to kick up our heels and divert energy from the immune system.

Specific Immunity

If the phagocytes are unable to rid the body of virus or bacteria, signals are transmitted to the lymphocytes, which function in a relatively specific manner. T-lymphocytes undergo maturation within the thymus gland and play multiple roles. Some are regulatory, in that they either can up-regulate or down-regulate other cells. They are referred to as helper or suppressor cells, respectively. Others, such as cytotoxic T-cells, are capable of directly killing a target.

137

Each has unique characteristics, which can be identified through the use of specific monoclonal antibodies. Hence, there are alternative sets of terminology used to describe these cells. They might be identified on the basis of their function, the type of surface marker they express, or the name of the antibody, which is used to identify the population.

T-cells, especially the less mature ones found in the thymus gland, are particularly susceptible to the inhibitory influence of cortisol. Since some of those cells will later regulate the biological activity of other lymphocytes, stress indirectly can impact on just about every aspect of your ability to fight disease. While high levels of cortisol are capable of down-regulating these cells, low levels are needed in order for them to function. Cortisol and catecholamines also are capable of triggering the migration of T-cells out of the thymus to the far reaches of the body, where they might be required.

Natural Killer Cells are large, granular, lymphocytes that lyse target cells, but without being previously sensitized. They play an important role in fighting a wide range of viral infections. B-lymphocytes remain in the bone marrow, where they undergo maturation. These cells will eventually differentiate into antibody-producing, plasma cells. Antibodies are proteins, which, ultimately, help to rid the body of microbes and other foreign molecules. Antibodies also are referred to as immunoglobulins, which is why the abbreviation is Ig. Like the T-cells, antibodies work in a relatively specific manner. Thus, the antibody that will protect you from influenza will not protect you from tetanus.

In response to most microbes, the first antibody to appear is IgM. It exists as a pentamer, or five molecules joined together. The levels build up quite rapidly, and because of the multiple, binding sites, IgM is highly efficient in combating infectious agents. On the other hand, its large size prevents it from

138

getting into all regions of the body, and it has a fairly short half-life.

That is not true of IgG, which is able to slip into most body regions due to its small size. It even crosses the placenta, providing adult levels of protection to the newborn. In addition, it has a relatively long half-life, enabling it to provide protection longer.

IgA exists primarily in secretions and in the colostrum of a mother's milk. Two molecules are joined, enabling it to latch efficiently onto microbes and, thereby, to prevent them from getting further into the body. One of the benefits of breast-feeding is the protection provided by the mother's IgA.

IgE is the antibody responsible for more absenteeism and discomfort than probably any other. That's because it links allergens, such as pollen and animal dander, to the surface of mast cells and basophils, thereby, giving rise to the symptoms of allergic reactions.

IgD is found in only trace amounts in the blood. It is, however, found on the surface of lymphocytes, where it may contribute to a microbe's binding site.

How To Stay Healthy

You need to understand that exposure to microbes is inevitable and that steps need to be taken to reduce the likelihood that the exposure will culminate in clinical symptoms. Optimal immunity can best be achieved through regular exercise, healthy sleep, and a balanced diet, conforming to the guidelines of the American Dietetic Association.

Avoid foods and beverages that may contain drugs capable of interfering with sleep. Caffeine is found in tea and coffee, as well as in many over-the-counter medications. It stimulates corticotrophin-releasing factor, thereby, triggering a hormonal stress cascade. That's not going to help you fall asleep. Furthermore, many sleep-promoting drugs can become addictive. In addition to the pharmacological changes induced by the ingestion of drugs, many have the potential for becoming behaviorally addictive. After weeks of associating the taking of a drug with falling asleep, it can become a conditioned stimulus. Now, without it, it's difficult to fall asleep.

Eating moderate portions of a well-balanced diet is paramount. For optimal immunity, it is especially important to get adequate amounts of vitamin C, which is required for wound healing as well as for normal functioning of phagocytes. Meet your nutritional needs by eating whole foods whenever you can. If you can't, choose options from a reputable company that maintains the highest possible standards.

If stress appears to be a factor in precipitating illness, use at least two approaches in dealing with the stress: one should focus upon the perception of events, and that would include cognitive techniques. If the perception that an event is threatening can be reduced, the physiological events will be, as well. At the same time, feedback signals capable of potentiating cognitive events need to be reduced. Deep breathing exercises, massage, and moderate exercise can be extremely helpful.

Moderate exercise in the aerobic zone for 30 minutes 3 to 5 times each week increases IL-1. This cytokine helps to stimulate T-cells as well as slow-wave sleep. Following exercise, the slow-wave, sleep-induced release of growth hormone helps to rebuild muscle. It also promotes a healthy immune system. It's one of many reasons why people who exercise moderately are healthier than those who don't.

Take steps to prevent infection. Drink plenty of water. Both the skin and mucous secretions require that you remain properly hydrated in order to function optimally.

Each of us needs enough sleep. That is the amount that enables us to awaken without artificial means, such as alarms or radios. In addition, we need sufficient delta or slow-wave sleep, which is when growth hormone is produced. Most delta sleep is experienced during the first half of the sleep cycle; so going to bed earlier than usual is better than sleeping in, if you want to provide optimal support to your immune system.

A well-tuned immune system can allow you to keep performing at your best under stressful situations, such as a tough argument with your teenager or discovering that your investments will be insufficient to sustain you in retirement. In some situations, you may have already been exposed to a virus, which can immediately start to negatively affect your abilities. But a fit immune system will not allow that to happen. Perhaps you're one of those people who can never shake a cold, while your co-worker never gets sick. A weak immune system may be the reason your health is so different, even though you each have the same exposure.

However, the immune system does considerably more than simply protect us from disease. Do you know that some forms of depression have now been linked with too much immunity? Or that chemicals produced by the immune system can affect your memory and reaction time? Even sleep and the ability to awaken feeling refreshed are linked with your immune system.

Yet, many people harm this important healing system because of the widely advertised belief that more is better.

This is an advertised belief, and it is not always true. It's all well and good to want more immunity if you've had chemotherapy, and your immune system has been derailed, or if you are highly susceptible to infections. Under these circumstances, you may very well want to take steps to boost your immune system. But, if you have any type of inflammatory disease, if you have any type of autoimmune problem, if you suffer from severe allergies, or if you have had a transplant, the last thing you want to do is try to boost your immune system. In fact, you may want to take steps to bring down your immune system, not to enhance it.

There is no question that many botanical products and herbs have the potential to serve as powerful medicines, not only in modulating the immune system, but also in affecting other physical and mental disorders. It's because many of them do work so well that you have to be aware of their downside. If a remedy can boost something, that's good if you need to be boosting that system. But, it could be bad if the system is working the way it should, and it is now thrown out of balance. Your immune system is a double-edged sword. You don't want too little because you will be susceptible to infections. But neither do you want too much. You need immunologic balance.

Here's also a behavioral option, which I strongly recommend. It will enhance the immune system when it's too low; it'll bring it down when it's too high, and it seems to have the wisdom to know what needs to be done. The intervention is 'eat less.' It's something many Native Americans figured out long before modern day scientists showed that reducing caloric intake would increase longevity. Not only that, but we know from the research of Dr. Robert Good that eating less will restore harmony to the immune system. He has demonstrated that it will help alleviate the symptoms of those susceptible to infections, as well as of those who are prone to autoimmunity. No, it will not make the diseases disappear. Instead, it renders the symptoms more manageable. It's not clear how this works, although a lot of people believe that it works by reducing free radicals. By decreasing overall metabolism, you are decreasing exposure to those oxidative metabolites, which have been linked with a large number of chronic illnesses.

Here's how you can take advantage of this information. Eat as much food as you need; eat it whenever you want, but when you reach the point when you don't need any more, but you still may want seconds or thirds, that's when you push the plate away. You leave the table feeling just a little bit hungry. And make sure that you eat dessert. That is important for three reasons. First, when you know dessert is coming, it's easier to push the plate away. Not only that, but it takes time to clear away the entrée and bring dessert to the table. During that time, there's a period when the signals from your stomach can get to your brain, signaling that you are full. A lot of people eat too quickly, and, by the time the signal gets to the brain saying, 'I'm full,' it's too late. You've already consumed 20 percent more food that you not only did not need, but that you also did not really want. Recognize, too, that dessert brings closure to the meal. It's the official end. And when you have that taste of the sweet flavor in your mouth, you are less inclined to want to rip another piece of flesh off of the carcass sitting by the fridge. No, I'm not suggesting that you gorge on ice cream. You can have fresh fruit. Or, it might be in the form of tea or coffee, but there needs to be a ritual that brings closure to the meal.

Nothing will interfere more with your pleasure and productivity than an infection. Here are some steps that you can take to decrease the probability of catching a cold, and, if you do get one, to have a speedier recovery.

Prevention, prevention, prevention. Without question, the best thing to do is to take steps to avoid exposure to cold-causing viruses. And that includes keeping your nose clean. Literally. Rhinovirus, one of the more common viruses that causes common cold symptoms, has got to get deep into the nasopharynx in order to trigger symptoms. This is the area where the nose and mouth come together. Unless it gets in there, it's not going to make you sick. The only way the virus can get there is through touch or through the air. Start by keeping your hands away from your nose and your eyes. Obviously, that's not going to put it into the area where it's going to cause problems, but a virus at the base of the nose is more likely to be inhaled. On average, most people's hands wander up to their eyes or noses at least once every three hours. If you simply train yourself to reduce this behavior, you will decrease the probability of catching a cold. Your awareness is the first step.

Wash your hands, especially when you are around other people who have colds. Shaking hands or touching the same surfaces that they have definitely will increase your probability of catching a cold. And move away from people who are sneezing or coughing. Common cold viruses are aerosols, which means they are transmitted through the air, where innocent bystanders can pick them up. There is no question that when people with colds take precautions by simply covering their noses and mouths before coughing and sneezing, they significantly reduce the probability of transmitting that virus to somebody else.

Make sure that you have plenty of vitamin C in your diet. While there is no evidence that vitamin C can prevent a cold, there is no question that adequate vitamin C in your diet is necessary to maintain a healthy immune system, and there is some suggestive evidence that it might be able to lessen the severity of symptoms and the duration of the cold once you get it. But keep the amount in the 70 to 90 mg range, which is recommended by the American Dietetic Association, since too much can cause problems.

Avoid surfaces where viruses may lurk. A cold virus may be able to survive for up to several hours after landing on a surface. You don't have to be obsessive about it, but if you see a lot of used tissues lying around in a telephone booth, find another phone to use or disinfect the mouthpiece before you put it close to your own mouth. Be careful when in fitness centers. People who are working out and perspiring are constantly wiping their faces and, perhaps, picking up a few viruses if they happen to be recovering from a cold. When they place their sweaty palms on the handholds of a treadmill, they are transferring that virus to the surface where you might pick it up. I'm not saying to stop working out. Just take extra precautions if you work out during flu season, and pay attention to who used the equipment before you.

Your immune system is your best weapon against viral infections. Don't waste your time or money taking antibiotics. All they'll do is destroy the good bacteria that reside in your G.I. system, resulting in stomach upset. The best things to do are drink lots of fluids and follow your body's cues to get plenty of bed rest. It's during slow-wave sleep that growth hormone is released, and that is a very powerful stimulant for the immune system. Go to bed an hour earlier than usual, and you'll get an extra dose of that healing sleep.

Eat chicken soup. It works especially if it's hot. A lot of microbes cannot survive higher than normal temperatures. So when that hot soup passes down your throat, you are creating a very inhospitable environment for those pathogens that happen to be lurking there. Furthermore, chicken, like most foods that contain protein, has an amino acid called cystine. This is released from the meat when the soup is prepared. It so happens there is a striking biochemical similarity between cystine and a drug called acetylcysteine, which is precisely what doctors prescribe for those people who have bronchitis and respiratory infections. Indeed, acetylcysteine was originally extracted from chicken feathers and skin. It thins the mucous in the lungs and facilitates its expulsion, which, of course, is going to take viruses with it. Add some hot peppers and spice, and you'll increase the beneficial effects. That's because peppers and hot curry powders can stimulate salivation in the mouth. This also helps to thin out the mucous, making it easier to expel. And don't forget to add a little garlic, which has natural anti-microbial properties.

Take care of those around you. Even though your foremost concern might be eliminating your own symptoms, you need to make sure your significant other does not get sick, or else he may not be able to prepare that hot soup or run down to the market to get the medications you need. Colds are most infectious during the first three days from when the first symptom appears. That's when you are transmitting a maximum number of viruses into the environment. By the fourth day, your risk to others is significantly reduced, even though you may still be experiencing symptoms. In fact, it probably will take a full two weeks to eliminate all the vestiges of a cold, but it's only during that first three-day period that you are most contagious.

Stay upbeat. Sheldon Cohen at Carnegie Mellon University in Pittsburgh has found that the more positive you are, the less likely you are to catch a cold in the first place. After you do experience symptoms, they will be less severe than those in people who have a less positive attitude. Rent humorous videos or read an upbeat novel. Talk to a friend—on the phone, of course, until you've passed through the most infectious stage. Social support does wonders for your health.

Eliminate dairy products if you have a cold. The protein in cow's milk can irritate the immune system of some people. Furthermore, milk products also are more likely to increase mucous production, which will increase congestion.

Make a steam tent by placing a towel over a pot of hot water and inhale the steam for a period of 10 minutes.

Add a quarter of a teaspoon of salt to one cup of warm water and gargle at least once every half hour until the symptoms of the sore throat are abated.

Allow a fever to run its course as long as it is not excessive. Many pathogens cannot survive when body temperature goes up.

Protecting the Immune System From Stress

While moderate exercise will fortify the immune system, intense exercise may do the opposite; the incidence of upper respiratory illness is very high in people who run marathons or engage in other forms of intense exercise. This is especially true during the two-week period following a race. It is suspected that the intense exercise depletes the body of vitamin C and glutamine, which, in turn, impairs the functioning of Natural Killer and Lymphokine-Activated Killer Cells. There is little rationale for equating emotional upheaval with running a marathon from an exercise perspective. There is a connection, however, from the standpoint of stress. While differing in origin, each gives rise to similar physiological events. For that reason, my recommendations for protecting the immune system during times of stress are based upon studies conducted using ultra-marathon runners.

147

A particularly well-designed study revealed that consumption of 600 mg of vitamin C for 3 weeks prior to a race resulted in a 68 percent reduction in the incidence of upper respiratory infection in athletes. A reduction in both the incidence of infection as well as in the number of symptom days was observed. This was not true of age-matched individuals who were not athletes. In other words, vitamin C appeared to be protective only when the body was under duress. While much has been published on the dangers of excessive vitamin C consumption, it appears to be safe for the relatively short duration of 3 weeks. In the study of ultra marathon runners, no deleterious effects were reported. Nonetheless, should this regimen be adopted, you should be aware that if the amount of vitamin C is too much, the initial symptoms will probably involve the gastrointestinal system. If that occurs, you should reduce the amount consumed since more serious harm could arise with continued consumption of large amounts of this vitamin.

You need to understand that there is no such thing as a good or a bad effect from a biological perspective. There is only an effect. What might be beneficial in one context may be very harmful in another. This is certainly the case with vitamin C. When exposed to a large amount of stress, there may be some benefits in consuming amounts, which exceed the levels recommended by nutritionists for the average person. This was clearly demonstrated in the study with ultra-marathon runners. However, under some circumstances, serious and deleterious side effects may result. In addition, whenever any medical intervention is being evaluated, it is necessary to be aware of not just the potential for benefits, but also the potential for detrimental side effects. Ultimately, the cost-benefit ratio must be weighed to determine what the best course might be.

In addition, supplements containing glutamine, a metabolic substrate and precursor for ribonucleotide synthesis, should be included in the diet in the event of long periods requiring intense activity. Plasma levels of glutamine decrease under such circumstances and so need to be replenished. This amino acid is particularly important since it plays a critical role during the course of a normal immune response. It is required for the production of cytokines, such as viral-fighting interferon and other chemical weapons needed to combat infection. It is one of the most prevalent amino acids in the body, with the primary source being skeletal muscle protein. Following intense exercise (stress), it becomes depleted and correlates with infection. Poor performance, chronic fatigue, and sleep disturbances also have been correlated with overtraining and decreased levels of glutamine.

A causal link between low levels of glutamine and down regulation of the immune system is not proven; however, this is strongly suggested by a study showing that 5 grams of L-glutamine in mineral water given immediately after and again 2 hours following a race resulted in a significant reduction in upper respiratory tract infections. 81 percent of those taking a placebo experienced symptoms, while only 49 percent of those taking the supplement did.

Another interesting observation suggests that the consumption of approximately 5 to 6 percent liquid carbohydrate is capable of attenuating the rise in cortisol and catecholamines, which normally occurs following intense exercise. It works by reducing the need for cortisol stimulation of glucose from stored glycogen. In addition, liquid carbohydrate was found to prevent the redistribution of immune system cells that normally occurs during exercise. Presumably, if stress has the potential of down regulating the immune system through excessive cortisol production, then ingestion of carbohydrate should be protective. On the other hand, a person suffering from inflammatory disease, which may be the consequence of too little cortisol, may be advised to do the opposite. Clearly, the means by which to modulate the immune system exists.

149

What is not clear are all of the clinical ramifications. The above-cited studies suggest that under conditions of extreme physical stress, supplements of vitamin C and glutamine may be protective. It's quite possible that they would be for individuals experiencing other forms of stress capable of diminishing the immune system.

Expectations, Beliefs, and Immunity

Finally, let's consider how beliefs can influence your immune system and health. Naturally, I'm referring to the placebo effect, which serves as the most convincing line of evidence that there is a link between the mind and the body. It is triggered by beliefs and expectations. The drug companies use it all the time. It's the reason different colors, tastes, and textures are used when marketing a particular drug. No, we should not ignore the concept of placebo. Instead, we should make full use of it. Here's an illustration of what I'm talking about.

Imagine you have never heard of an herbal remedy recently introduced to the US market. Experts claim, "This product, if taken according to our instructions, will cure your arthritis, multiple-sclerosis, allergies, and keep you from catching colds and flu." Elsewhere in the brochure are personal testimonials from patients and claims by doctors.

How is this advertised claim likely to influence you? If you're a skeptic, then your response might wisely be, "This is too good to be true." (*This is probably a correct assumption. Allergy and arthritis are examples of too much immunity. Colds and other infections are manifestations of too little. A single formulation couldn't aid both types of conditions.*) On the other hand, the image created by these words may increase your expectations that the product will do the same for you. It might, but, be careful. You want to be sure that any benefits are due to the ingredients and not to just your

150

belief. Be objective, and follow the protocol that I've described in the next chapter to make sure it's really working. Even then, realize that there are probably other factors involved. There are as many possibilities for why improved health can occur as there are factors which can influence it. You'll never know for sure whether what you take is really responsible for the outcome. Nor can you be sure that it wasn't. That's why you should remain open-minded and collect your own data.

I overheard while taking a break from a lecture tour one of the most honest assessments of how remedies work from a homeopath in London. I'd stopped in to look around her shop. While there, an elderly lady came in, very agitated. She marched to the counter with her big, shopping bag, pulled out a half-empty vial of medicine, slammed it on the counter, and loudly declared, "*This medicine has not helped my arthritis at all. In fact, I knew it wasn't going to help when I bought it. I knew I was wasting my money. It may have made my arthritis even worse, so I would like my money back, please.*" And the shopkeeper responded by saying, "*Mrs. Jones, with that attitude, I'm not surprised the medicine didn't work. It's a homeopathic medicine. It can't work by itself. You have to help it. Now, I want you to change your attitude. I want you to take what's left of this medicine, think positively about it, believe in it, and if it still doesn't work, then I will give you your money back. But, you change your attitude first, so it can do what it's supposed to do.*" And Mrs. Jones got very flustered. She said, "*Yes, of course, you're right. I'm sorry,*" and off she went.

How I wished I could have tape-recorded that exchange because that homeopath was being honest. She was acknowledging what everyone who dispenses any type of medicine should acknowledge. Nothing is working for a single reason. One of the most enduring pathways to optimal health is your belief. Use it to enhance the other things you might be doing.

BECAUSE I'M SKEPTICAL

We are constantly being subjected to advertised, cultural, or hand-me-down beliefs that sound good, but there's always that nagging question: "*Is it right for me?*" A darned good question because what may be a perfect solution for one person, may be a disaster for someone else. We are hung up on statistics when the time comes to evaluate medical advice. If the FDA proclaims that an effect is significant after all the proper tests, we have a tendency to embrace the belief that the protocol will do the same for us. It's not that simple. Nothing pertaining to health is. First, what the statistics assume is that everyone in the study is basically the same. In other words, they are chosen on the basis that they represent the average person in a particular category. Second, the majority of the people respond in the desired way. But what if you are not average? What if you are a part of the minority for whom the protocol may be harmful?

Let's consider the opposite scenario, where an intervention is rejected because the majority does not experience a beneficial effect. Could you be a member of the smaller group for whom the protocol might be just what you are looking for to improve your health and happiness?

And what about all the options that are now available, but because they are not regulated, do not have to be tested at all? How can you tell if those are things you should be doing? It's not easy to answer these questions. That's because there are so many variables influencing health. Nonetheless, there is some information you should be armed with so that you can make an informed decision. Furthermore, you can do what scientists do, and use your body as a laboratory.

How To Tell If It's Right For You

You'll begin by doing some background research. In this case, it's about yourself, and what better place to start than with your relatives. After all, they gave you your genes, which served as the architectural plans with which to construct your body. If there were a glitch, you might be able to find out in order to take steps to avoid experiencing the same fate.

Next, you'll need to assess your resources. In other words, what have you got to work with? What equipment is at hand, and what shape is it in? (I'm referring to you and your level of fitness.)

Then you'll formulate some questions or hypotheses for testing. Of the large number of topics I could have chosen, I picked one that is near and dear to not only me, but to an estimated 60 percent of the US population who patronize the rapidly growing health food industry. I won't give you any recipes, though, because one size doesn't fit all. Instead, I'll arm you with information that you need to have as you consider which options you are going to test.

And, finally, I'll tell you how to design the experiment. You'll be the guinea pig, so pay attention. Let's start with your background.

Great progress is being made in mapping the human genome. Eventually, it is hoped that a better understanding of the genetic blueprint will enable doctors to predict who is susceptible to certain diseases and then implement strategies to head off the symptoms at the pass. That's the intent. In reality, many people will experience other types of problems stemming from anxiety as they worry that the genetic code will become a self-fulfilling prophecy. This already is happening as people poke around and ask questions about their parents' health. It's needless worry, first and foremost, because genes do not cause a problem. They influence probability. Yes, you should take genetic-based information seriously, not because you need something else to worry about, but because there probably will be steps that you can take to minimize the likelihood of an undesirable outcome.

Let's keep things in perspective. All disease is multi-factorial. There is no single factor that predicts the progression of any illness. Contracting an illness is similar to playing the lottery. Let's consider, as an example, the common cold, which requires a number of factors to be in place before you will experience any symptoms. Yes, your immune response genes are very important. They determine how well your immune system is likely to function to ward off the symptom-inducing virus. Unless you are exposed to the pathogen, though, it really makes no difference what your immune response genes look like. You also need to have a number of biological factors in place. For example, the way you handle stress can influence how well you fight an infection. The quality of your sleep can alter your levels of growth hormone, which, in turn, can regulate the growth of white cells. And let's not forget diet. After all, every aspect of your viral-fighting, cellular army needs proper nourishment. You also can bolster your immune system through the judicious use of exercise.

These are just some of the factors that play a role. Not mentioned are all the psychological variables such as personality, coping style, perception, and belief. Having a genetic predisposition for a type of illness is rather like buying a lottery ticket and having one of 5 winning numbers when you purchase it. It means very little unless you have all of the other correct numbers. That rule applies whether you are dealing with infection, depression, pessimism, or just about anything else pertaining to your body. That doesn't mean that you should ignore your family tree. Far from it. It's very important to pay attention so that you can take steps to offset its potential impact upon your health. Start by putting yourself into

155

historical perspective. And the best way to do that is by asking pertinent questions.

Determining Your Genetic Risk

Begin with your parents. Half your genetic make-up came from your mother, while the remainder came from your father. They are teachers who have walked in shoes very close to your size. You have received not just their genes, but chances are your beliefs as well, including those that impact your dietary and exercise habits. Yes, by examining your past, you can get a glimpse into your future. With the right information, you may be able to take several steps to defuse potential time bombs. Start with the environment, and ask them about their health habits.

Ask, *"Did you care about your health while growing up?"* If your mother grew up in Love Canal and worked in a PCB factory, then her breast cancer probably was environmentally triggered. Likewise, if your father had an identification complex with the Marlboro Man, and his only exercise was opening a Budweiser, then you probably can avoid his fate of experiencing a heart attack by taking steps to avoid that lifestyle. Inquire about eating habits. Did your folks eat broccoli and fish, or were they weighted down with cheeseburgers and fries? It's surprising the number of serious diseases now linked with diet, sedentary behavior, and other life-style factors. Those are the things about which you can do something. On the other hand, if your parents ate all the right foods, exercised, and possessed good, stress-coping skills, their maladies may have been due in large part to a genetic predisposition. All the more reason for you to take steps to adopt an even healthier lifestyle to counteract that potential factor you may have inherited.

Next, ask about their medical file. What were their blood pressure, cholesterol count, and resting heart rate? By themselves, these numbers don't mean much. But if you can rule out a diet that by all rights should have turned their cardiovascular systems into a Jiffy Lube, then you need to be wary of having a genetic predisposition to the same, underlying conditions. Even better, get a copy of your folks' medical files, and share it with your doctor. Chances are, he or she will pick up other data, along with critical information regarding its interpretation. You also might want to check out where they stored their fat. If it was around the midsection, rather than the hips, and you follow suit, then your risk of heart disease increases.

Ask about their vision. Glaucoma is hereditary and treatable. Knowing that you might be susceptible would warrant regular screenings since this condition is treatable, if detected early. Once damage has been done, though, it's too late. While glaucoma can be prevented, damage to the optic nerve cannot be repaired.

You also might have inherited your behavior. Fathers, especially, motivate many men, so it's important to know what your father's beliefs and values were. Some men hold back, not wanting to compete with their dads; others fear never measuring up, while others go into competitive mode. Chances are, you won't change your style, but, at least, being aware of where your style came from may help you understand it better. This also applies to how your parents dealt with stress. Did they repress anger or vent it? Chances are, you follow the same pattern. Internalizing anger is not only damaging to your heart; it is damaging to your immune system, as well.

Not all genetic information is learned from parents. Newspaper articles often sacrifice accuracy for the sake of clarity, so make sure that you don't jump to erroneous conclusions and experience sleepless nights because of a hastily penned sentence on the back page of your newspaper.

My recommendation is to use published information to heighten your awareness of a potential problem. Then examine your family tree, but only as far back as your grandparents. What happened before that has become so dilute that it's not worth worrying about. Instead, concentrate on siblings, cousins, aunts, and uncles. Look for similar conditions in blood relatives on the same side of the family that cannot be explained by lifestyle. If your mother's brother and maternal grandmother both had strokes in their 40's, then take steps to protect yourself from a similar fate. On the other hand, if your mother's mother and father's sister had breast cancer, because they were not related to each other, I wouldn't be overly concerned about the role of chromosomes.

Evaluating Medical Claims

From now on, whenever you are presented with an advertised belief promoting a new and improved version of dietary advice, you will have the definitive test at your disposal. Before you begin, you'll need a heart rate monitor, a watch, and access to either a bicycle ergo meter or treadmill with an odometer attached.

The routine will always be the same. Warm up until your heart rate reaches 75 percent of the maximum. This is the moderate stress range. Then, note the time, and keep your heart rate as close to that level as you can for exactly five minutes. You are going to measure two variables: 1) the distance traveled during the five-minute test, and 2) the time it takes for your heart rate to return to 50 percent of the maximum. Make every attempt to keep the conditions exactly the same each time you take this test. This is especially important with respect to the warm up and cool down phase of the regimen. You also should note your fluid consumption and medications.

First, take this test after following your normal routine. Then, follow the guidelines suggested in the advertised belief promoting the supplement you're considering. It might be a combination of things. Repeat the test, and compare the results. By the way, you could use virtually any exercise for this test. The reason stationary fitness equipment is recommended is because weather is not a factor. As a result of consuming health-promoting foods or supplements, your entire body should function at a greater level of efficiency. At the same heart rate, you will be able to cover a greater distance, and your heart rate will recover faster. Use this test to evaluate your performance at different times of the day or after a variety of different foods.

Remember, exercise is a form of physical stress. Consequently, you actually are testing the effects of supplements upon your ability to perform and to recover from stress. What works during exercise also will serve you well in the office, negotiating with your teenager, or dealing with the myriad of daily stressors that are simply unavoidable. No, the test is not perfect. Each time you do this brief workout, there will be a modest training effect, which might confound your measures. So vary the sequence, and then repeat certain regimens to control for circadian, monthly, or seasonal effects.

You can use a similar process to evaluate other claims. For example, establish a scale from 1 to 10 for whatever it is you want to improve. Sleep, perhaps? Then establish 1 as the equivalent of awakening in a coma and 10 with wanting to run a marathon. The other numbers would be correlated with intermediate states. Each morning, for at least a week before following any protocols, keep score. Then, put your notes in a drawer. Start a new page as you begin the protocol. After a week, take out your baseline data, and compare the results. Was there an improvement with no side effects? Then keep doing it. No change? Then save your money, or try something else. And you can apply this procedure to virtually anything that you want to improve--from memory enhancement to athletic prowess.

It's your body, and it's different from everyone else's. Be leery of any protocol that is promoted as a one size fits all solution. It's highly unlikely that what would be suitable for a sedentary, middle-aged man with diabetes would be appropriate for a woman who is a tri-athlete. Even your body changes over time as I explained earlier. So what works in the summer may not do the same thing to your winter chemistry. Use common sense, and always question the interpretation of data as well as the beliefs to which they give rise. Use your body as a laboratory, and make sure it's right for you.

BECAUSE I CAN'T DO IT ALONE

What resources do you have available to achieve your goals? Other people are best. There's no question that the most devastating events are those involving the loss of a relationship. It might be in the form of a divorce, death of a family member, or retirement, which for some people may be a severance from their sole source of social support. While being alone can sometimes be helpful, there is an important difference between choosing to be alone and being isolated from others. You can be isolated from people when you are with them, and you can feel connected to people in your life while you are spending time alone. When you are under stress, social isolation can be very harmful to your well-being. You are more likely to dwell on the belief that no one else understands what you feel...or that you are worthless, flawed, or simply a bad person. As these feelings cascade, you soon find yourself feeling even more isolated and upset.

How Good Are You At Seeking Support?

Do you believe that it is a sign of weakness to ask others for help? Have you always been on your own? Do you think people will not like you if you expose your weaknesses? Many people do not have meaningful contact with others because they have never learned how to make themselves open and vulnerable in relationships. This keeps them distant from people. This is not to say that it is necessary or even healthy to run to others whenever you experience the slightest problem. Instead, recognize the opportunities to give and receive emotional support from others. Draw on the wisdom that others can offer.

Some people create personal barriers to helpful, meaningful relationships. Because of unhealthy beliefs, they may go to great lengths to avoid contact with others in certain circumstances. You may be outgoing in the workplace, where your role in the hierarchy is well-defined, but you may be ill at ease at a party. Or the contacts that you do have may not be genuine. If there are circumstances under which you have difficulty communicating with others, is it due to one of the following beliefs?

- I will look silly or intrusive.
- I will be seen as making sexual overtures.
- I am unworthy to be speaking to that person.

If any of these beliefs ring true to you, apply the same questions used to probe other beliefs:

- Are these your beliefs or those of someone else?
- Are your beliefs based upon experience?
- Can you think of times in your life when your belief was challenged by reality?
- Have your beliefs ever kept you from achieving a goal?
- Are certain themes reflected in your beliefs?
- Are you willing to change one or more of your beliefs if they are obstacles to your goals?
- Are your beliefs serving a useful purpose?

When you do make contact with others in your life, let them know what you need from them. Don't expect them to read your mind. Some people intuitively will know how to support you; others will not. Some people will try to give advice, while others will talk about their own problems, and some will try to cheer you up.

While these responses can be helpful, it is better to talk with someone who knows how to listen. Often, what you need most when distressed is someone who can listen without judging. Another person doesn't have to solve your problem, but simply hear you out. This provides you with an

162

opportunity to express your thoughts and emotions, something that is extremely important when you are feeling distressed. If you don't have a partner, a family member, or a friend who can do this, you might want to talk with a professional - a therapist. The key is talking with someone who will allow you to express your feelings in order to work through them.

And don't forget to reciprocate. No one is devoid of hardship. Become a resource for those friends you depend upon. The following guidelines will greatly enhance your listening skills. Chances are, you do them automatically when listening to someone you care about.

- Focus upon the other person's words and body language.
- Show interest by moving your eyebrows in response to what is being said.
- Use facial gestures, such as a smile, to convey empathy.
- Seek clarification when appropriate.
- Summarize what you have heard.

Unfortunately, relationships can sometimes be a reason you never get around to doing the things you need to do. Some people are manipulative, deceptive, or overly controlling. Such relationships – personal, professional, or otherwise - can take a serious toll on your motivation if you find yourself on the receiving end of these tactics. You'll enable others to accomplish their goals, but you'll never achieve yours. If you answer *yes* to any of the following questions, you need to take steps to modify your response to other people.

- Have you ever purchased something that you didn't really want?
- Have you ever accepted a food or beverage item when you didn't want to?
- Have you ever agreed to do something that was counter to your value system?

- Have you ever regretted not taking action?
- Now think about why you responded the way you did.
- What beliefs allowed you to be manipulated?
- What beliefs kept you from holding your ground or speaking your mind?
- If someone wanted you to do something that was against your will, how best would that person accomplish his goal?

Reflecting upon the answers to these questions will help you to identify the problem. Now, here's how you set about fixing it. A very simple strategy is to employ acting skills. Recall that occasion when you did speak your mind, and you met your objective. Reflect upon an occasion involving similar circumstances when you were able to do what you believed was right. Create a screenplay, and practice. Practice, practice, and practice. Hear your words, and watch your posture and movement. You will become what you believe you are. By recreating the behaviors associated with success, you will drive the physiology of success. It will happen. But this is something that has to be learned, and learning requires practice.

The rules for dealing with relationship problems are quite involved and have to be tailored for each situation. Nonetheless, here are some general guidelines.

- Do what you believe is right, not what is expected.
- Your choices are always yes, no, or none of the above.
- You don't have to give a reason for your choice.
- You don't have to apologize for your choice.
- Take some time – even sleep on it before deciding.
- Watch for signs of deception.
- Recognize your vulnerability.

Why is this so important? It is because if you are doing things to please others, then you are not likely to be pursuing your personal goals.

Dealing with Difficult People

Let's examine specific examples of how you might better cope with people who are keeping you from doing the things you need and want to be doing. Pay more attention to the strategy and less to the specific example. The approach could be applied to the home setting, work setting, or just about any social situation where you might encounter the individual described.

Belligerent People. Let's begin with the belligerent supervisor who rules through intimidation. You have no idea when the temper tantrum is going to occur, but you can be absolutely certain that an episode will take place very soon. Most important of all is that you do not act helpless. If you cower in fear, you are playing the classic role of a victim. If you respond by yelling back, you have lost control of your own emotions, and you are allowing your response to be manipulated by the other individual. Your job is to be rational, deal with the situation in a constructive way, and continue to be the mature person you are. A tall order, I know, when someone is verbally attacking you. Your first response may be an increase in your heart rate and respiration rate. The latter are classic stress responses associated with anger and fear, the two emotions most likely to be elicited.

A good way to counter these physiological responses is by concentrating on your breathing. Take a deep breath, exhale slowly, and, as you are doing this, remind yourself that the outburst is not about you personally but about something that you have done or has been perceived. Focus on what the individual is saying to determine whether or not there is anything useful in his outburst. If a lot of the information that is being stated is a personal attack, or if it's information that has no value, then you need to actively stop the attack. Here are some guidelines -- but recognize that you need to mold your response so that it fits with your personality and with the personality of the person with whom you are dealing.

Ask the person to please stop, and very calmly inform him that you do not appreciate being treated in this manner. You are conveying a very clear, concise message, which is not threatening; and, at the same time, is not a defensive posture, but it is a response that puts you firmly in control.

State simply that you want a time-out. If the person is speaking so loudly that he can't hear you, place the palm of your hand over your fingers of the other hand in the same manner that a player in a professional sport would do to signal to the referees that a time-out is being sought. That gesture, by itself, can distract the individual long enough that the message may be conveyed. Then make it clear that you do want to hear what it is that is being said, but that you need to have the person slow down. Don't ask him to calm down, which could be perceived as a criticism. However, asking him to slow down conveys that you really want to hear what he has to say. This, in itself, can calm the individual, while decreasing the probability that you will send him into another spiral of rage by having expressed criticism.

Agree with the attacker. Acknowledge that the problem is serious and needs to be discussed. However, it has to be done on rational terms, not emotional terms. That message can be communicated very subtly when you say, "*Let's talk about this. You start, and while you are describing to me your view of the problem, I will not interrupt. And when you're finished, I would like an opportunity to pose any questions I might have.*" By engaging in this kind of response, you are firmly in control and are serving in the capacity of a mediator. You have assured the individual that

166

you are interested in what he has to say, and you have guaranteed a period of time during which he will not be interrupted. This, in itself, can have an overall calming effect. At the same time, you are listening to the valid concerns being expressed by the individual. You also need to be studying them, and then evaluate why it is that he is saying what he is saying.

Back Stabbers. There are some people who will greet you with a smile and say some of the sweetest things in your presence, but the second that you are out of sight will go out of their way to stab you in the back. Chances are such an individual has very low self-esteem and is, in his own mind, elevating his stature by criticizing those he perceives to be superior. You probably are not the only victim of such a person, so a group response may be in order. Identify others who are being manipulated in the same way. This shouldn't be too difficult because the back-stabber is probably undermining them in your presence. Initially, go along with the game. Pretend that everything is fine, and suggest that everyone gather for a social function, such as lunch or dinner after work. Then get your colleagues to agree to state the same message. This can be done in different ways, but the message is - we need to improve working conditions, and this means you have to stop voicing your concerns to people other than the one who can do something.

It's quite likely that this type of individual is going to say all sorts of pleasant things and will make excuses and false promises. He may even deny what you know to be true. Chances are you are not going to change this person. It's very difficult to change a person's personality. But you may convince this individual that you and your colleagues are not the ones who should be targeted for this type of manipulation. The consequence will be that the back-stabber will look for other targets and, at least, leave you alone. It is important that

167

you remain calm, maintain eye contact with the individual, interject no emotion, and simply repeat the message, which, modified to fit your circumstances, is, *"You must stop this behavior."*

Crisis Seekers. These people seem to have an enormous amount of energy. They are extremely focused on what they do, but only when it has reached the point of a crisis. Often, the crisis they are attending to has absolutely nothing to do with what they are supposed to be doing. His child has become ill, or her furnace suddenly has malfunctioned. Perhaps the car is in the shop, which demands the person's total attention. The consequence is that their contribution to achieving the goal is not being made. Your mission in dealing with such people is to approach on the level of their belief and to make sure they perceive what they are supposed to be doing as a crisis. In this way, such people do what is expected of them.

For example, explain to such individuals how desperate it is that they mobilize their energy and come through for you. Interject as much drama as you can in describing how terrible the consequences will be if the job or the project is not completed on time. Be careful not to be critical of them. If they end up feeling rejected or inferior, then it will become their crisis. You need to be prepared to use this technique continuously. There is nothing wrong with such individuals' basic behavior. You just want them to interject the same enthusiasm and energy into helping you stay on course.

Invalidators. Another type of difficult person is the invalidator. These are people who are constantly finding things to criticize. They don't have temper tantrums, but their continuous criticism eventually eats away at your self-esteem. Often, these people are perfectionists, and they engage in what psychologists refer to as dichotomous thinking. They believe that if one, small mistake is made, then everything is wrong.

You may have spent a week or more working on a special project, and the invalidator will come in, take one look at it, and say that it is absolute rubbish. Well, that's highly unlikely. There may be some component that needs some adjustment, but the entire effort is unlikely to be without some merit. The best way to deal with this individual is to get control of your breathing in order to make sure that your physiology doesn't cause you to lose control. Then reflect on the fact that you did spend a lot of time working on the task, doing the best job that you could. Next, sit down with the person, most likely a supervisor, and ask them to tell you what part of the project is causing the most concern. In this way, you're not ignoring their comment, nor are you denying the essence of their criticism. Instead, you are getting them to single out what is probably the genuine problem. By doing this, you can set about to remedy it.

Ostracizers. The final type of difficult person is the one who employs ostracism to control others. They make it difficult for you to do the job that you are supposed to be doing because they fail to pass along information you need to do the job effectively. Often times, these people like to feel a sense of power, and, by excluding you from committees or the so-called 'in group,' they feel that they have elevated their own status. If this type of individual is the primary source of your stress and burnout, seek out a colleague who is a friend or who you know to be cooperative. Just make certain that this individual also is a member of the so-called 'in group' and a person the ostracizer happens to respect. Ask that person to make sure that important and relevant information be passed on to you. Don't mention the fact that you are being ostracized. Why bring attention to a problem if it's not necessary? What you need is the information that you are being denied. This strategy will enable you to accomplish that goal and to do your job by going around the difficult person.

When people are critical of someone else, especially when it is an unjustified and highly emotional attack, those individuals are revealing more about their own personality than they are about that of their victim. People tend to project their own attributes, especially the negative ones, onto others. At the same time, they frequently will engage in the very behaviors they find most disconcerting. This can be very useful to know if you want eventually to influence their behavior. It can reveal to you what they are most likely to react to. The key here is not to use this information to get revenge. Rather, use it to help them realize how troublesome their words or actions can be. They also are providing you with subtle clues helping to identify their own unmet needs.

Before proceeding, I want you very carefully to examine your relationships, and, in particular, the role your belief has and may continue to play in those relationships. Ponder these questions:

- Do you tend to gravitate towards individuals who are most like you or who are different? Why?
- Are your criteria for friendship based more upon physical or behavioral characteristics? Why?
- Do most of your friends come from contacts your spouse has made, or through your own connections? What is the reason for this?
- Are there certain types of people you avoid getting close to? Why?
- What role do your beliefs and values play as you make choices about associating with others?

Friends and family can be your greatest asset in progressing toward a goal, or your greatest obstacle. Chances are you can't isolate yourself from those who may be making life difficult. However, you can change your response and attitude so that their tactics do not undermine you.

Healing Relationships

Most of us believe that our friends are conduits to pleasure, a means by which to experience joy and happiness. That they are. But our relationships with others also can improve our mental and physical health. We may not think of social support as being a behavioral intervention, but this is exactly what it is. Caring contact between people not only is emotionally pleasurable, it promotes good health. Loneliness is as much a risk factor for disease as is high cholesterol or smoking. Friends also can help us sustain our motivation as well as assist along the way as we pursue our goals.

Unfortunately, in today's plugged-in world, with e-mail, faxes, cell phones, and beepers, many of us unplug in times of stress and isolate ourselves from what is one of the most valuable resources we have. Chronic stress, whether it be dealing with an impossible boss, the lingering illness of a loved one, or continual worry over paying the bills, can have a serious impact upon both the mind and the body. Often, as a result of such unrelenting pressure, we lose our ability to respond and slip into a sense of hopelessness and helplessness.

A classic study performed by researchers at Stanford University revealed that the hormonal response of monkeys to stress varied, depending upon the amount of social support they had available. Just providing contact with familiar animals significantly reduced cortisol, which is released during stress and is linked with memory loss, diabetes, impaired immunity, and heart disease. In short, friends were the best medicine.

It has long been known that social support promotes health in humans, probably via the same hormonal changes measured in the monkeys. Socialization probably helps diminish the release of potentially harmful chemicals within the body. If you are happily married, or if you have a large network of friends, you

171

have a greater life expectancy than do single people or those who have very few friends. In fact, people who have large networks of friends also have reduced risk of accidents and a lower incidence of just about all forms of illness.

Of course, some people are not highly social beings. Like Lucy in *Peanuts*, you may say, *"I love mankind; it's people I can't stand."* If you are a person like Lucy, who is not a highly social being, if you truly prefer a fairly reclusive lifestyle, or if you recently are divorced and relishing the sense of freedom, don't worry! Pets make an excellent social support group. A field of study known as human-animal bonding has revealed that people who have pets have lower blood pressure, in general, than people who do not. And when animals are present in long-term care facilities and nursing homes, patients tend to recover faster from surgical procedures and are more compliant about taking their medications.

We know that some people form attachments to their animals every bit as strong as the emotional bond between a parent and child. While there are many, beneficial effects to this emotional bonding, it may simply be that the benefits are derived from the sense of order a pet creates. Feeding the animal is a reminder to eat. Walking the dog brings us exercise, as well. Caring for the pet's health, such as that daily dose of heartworm medicine, is a reminder to take our own medications. Instead of saying that having animals is good for us, we should say the benefit arises from engaging in the behaviors associated with having animals around.

But what if you're a solitary sort who's also allergic to many animals? Does this mean your emotions will be so deprived that you're a magnet for illness and injury? No. Odd as it may seem, caring for plants works as well. It's a tough concept to explain on the basis of love and bonding, but studies do prove that the connection produces benefits. Judy Rhodin, while at Yale University, conducted studies in which plants were placed in hospital patients' rooms. In some rooms, only the hospital staff cared for the plants. In other rooms, the patients were asked to look after the plants, to water them, and to move them into and out of the sunlight. Those patients who tended to the plants had speedier, less complicated recoveries than those who did not.

The big question is, what does a plant, an animal, and a spouse all have in common? People who are recently divorced might suggest a number of things - and not all too pleasant. But, in the context of this concept, the key word appears to be *responsibility, responsibility* for a plant, a pet, and for a loved one. We can take this one step further. Accepting responsibility for your own health is a behavioral intervention that is conducive to a state of good health. This is why it can be detrimental to take *care of* someone else - you are treating them as though they are helpless. Instead, it is better to *care for* the person.

There is a vast difference between caring for and taking care of someone. When you care *for* another person, you are in partnership with that person. When you take care *of* someone, the implication is that he cannot take care of himself. It is proper to take care of an injured animal or a newborn infant. Yet, as that child grows and matures, it is important for that child to participate actively in his own care. When you deny the child the opportunity to acquire those skills, you increase the probability of a dependent relationship being established. Through the process of accepting responsibility, we each gain control over our own health.

Reducing Stress Through Friends

Equally important for your health and emotional well-being is your ability to express yourself. Putting your emotions into words allows you to perceive them from a new perspective. And, sometimes, altering the words we use alters our emotional response to past or present events. We call this sharing of emotional feelings *disclosure* – and it has been proven to be highly therapeutic, leading to long-term gains in well-being. For example, under well-controlled conditions, undergraduate college students were asked to recall the most traumatic event in their lives. One group narrated only the factual occurrences of the event, with no mention of their feelings about it. A second group described both the event and their feelings. A control group was asked to simply state what they were wearing at the time of the event or some other circumstantial element that had no emotional connotation.

Those people who recalled their feelings about the events experienced an initial episode of increased anxiety as well as a decline in their immune systems. But over the course of the semester, it was the members of the group recalling their feelings whose immune systems actually were more robust, requiring fewer visits to the student health center. There was something about the process of talking about the experience that was emotionally therapeutic and had a beneficial impact upon the immune system's ability to rebound. So much for the cultural belief that emotions are inherently bad and are the opposite of reason. It would be hard to prove, but I suspect many adults who have difficulty expressing emotions may have overheard as children an influential person say, *"Don't be so emotional. Be more reasonable."*

How does disclosure of emotions work? Several explanations have been offered. Among the most plausible is that when speaking or writing about a problem, it forces you to slow down. Information, which has been ricocheting around the emotional brain, is delayed during its translation into language. The problem then is perceived through different sensory pathways: the eyes and the kinesthetic senses in the case of written disclosure, or the ears in the case of oral disclosure. Each form also takes time, adding a third modality. As a result, your mind often finds it easier to recognize potential solutions

174

to improve or to overcome the perceived obstacle to getting things done.

Desensitization is another hypothesized possibility. Through the repetitive act of expressing your feelings, either on paper or by talking about them, the emotional edge eventually wears off. It's like watching re-runs of the same television program over and over again. You are able to distance yourself from their impact. Realize you are tinkering with the human mind, which doesn't always respond in the way we might want it to. Rehashing a problem may fuel the passion or serve as a constant reminder that the problem is still there. But, for the most part:

- Language provides a means of emotional expression.
- Language allows you to express emotions in a controllable format.
- Putting your emotions into words allows you to perceive them from a new perspective.
- Simply altering the words you use can alter your emotional response to past or present events.

Make certain you confide in a close friend who's a good listener and who will keep your confidences in trust. If your friends tend to be Type-A personalities, who get impatient waiting for you to spit it out or assume that you expect a list of ways to fix the problem, then you may need to seek the skills of a professional therapist. It's true that this can be expensive, but a good one is worth his or her weight in gold. Not only does a professional therapist have the skills to help you identify the true source of your problem, he or she also has the training to provide guidelines on how to resolve your issues.

Spiritual Resources

Spirituality is largely overlooked in the healing process because it is difficult to measure using the accepted criteria of Western medicine. Even defining the concept of spirituality is no trivial matter.

Ancient Greek philosophers equated spirituality with the mind. Spirit was the basis for emotion, and it was felt that harmony, or balance, between the spirit and the body was essential for good health. In more modern times, spirituality tends to be equated with religion, and words such as *faith, hope,* and *love* are used to describe it. It is important to recognize, though, that spirituality isn't necessarily equivalent to religion. You can base your life upon spiritual values without adhering to the doctrine of an organized religious group.

Spirituality can be defined as an intangible force which enables us to cope with life's challenges. This force can come from a belief in God, another external, guiding force, or from resources within the inner self. Spirituality is the source of hope and the purpose behind events which guide us. It is also the process through which we seek harmony with an unseen order of things.

For whatever reason, being involved with organized religion apparently can promote health. Psychiatrist David Larson cited a variety of research on the healing effect of religiosity. Here are some highlights:

- People who received strength or comfort from religion were less likely to die within six months of undergoing elective open-heart surgery than those who did not.

- A 10-year study of 2,700 people revealed that church attendance was the only social attribute correlating to lowered mortality rates.

- For women recovering from hip fractures, there was less depression and increased ability to walk greater distances in those with stronger religious beliefs and practices.

Although cause-and-effect is difficult to prove with these provocative findings (after all, you have to be reasonably healthy to attend religious ceremonies), religious associations do provide an opportunity for socialization and altruistic efforts, as well as greater spiritual awareness - all of which have been well documented to have health-promoting effects.

The possibility of divine intervention certainly cannot be ignored, although it would be exceedingly difficult to prove or disprove. An underlying assumption in science is that if a phenomenon cannot be measured or reproduced, it does not exist. While a reliance on such criteria is sometimes necessary; at the same time, it causes many people to summarily dismiss potentially effective interventions. Personally, I believe that absence of evidence should not be construed as evidence of absence. Just because scientists are not able to measure something, it does not mean it should be ignored. Nor should it be blindly embraced. Always remain open-minded and continuously gather all available information to formulate your beliefs.

Let's consider altruism as an example of these opposing views. Theologians would quote the Sermon on the Mount as a biblical endorsement of altruism; and, for many people of faith, this is all that's needed to accept the concept. Yet, biologists would evoke the argument and calculations of geneticist John Haldane. Haldane mathematically determined that a person should be willing to give up his or her life for two siblings or eight first cousins, as this would be in the individual's self-interest for preservation of their gene pool. Whether altruism has been impressed through spiritual assumptions or through biological mandate, it has been concluded that people who engage in some sort of altruistic pursuit have a greater life expectancy compared with those people who do not.

There are other, more immediate, benefits to be derived from acts of altruism. In a survey of 3,000 people, those who worked directly with others reported fewer incidences of headache, back pain, and stomachache. They had fewer symptoms associated with infections, such as colds and flu, and reported less inflammatory disease, such as arthritis. Also, many reported that during their time as volunteers, their eating and sleeping habits improved. It is interesting to note that many reported what can best be termed as *helper's high* - a feeling of euphoria which bears a striking resemblance to the state of well-being experienced by dedicated athletes due to the release of exercise-induced endorphins.

Love is another word that often comes to mind when speaking of spirituality. It is defined partly as placing more value upon another person's needs than our own. Here again, the element of social interaction comes into play. Everything I have described pertaining to altruism and social support explains the potential benefits of love. Two psychologists at the University of Arizona released a report based on surveys of interviews conducted with undergraduate students during the 1950's who were then interviewed again 35 years later. Looking for a connection between participants' past and present health, the researchers noted that those students who had rated their parents as highly loving showed levels of disease far lower than among those who had given their parents low ratings. After ruling out all other factors which might explain correlations with disease later in life, the only element that remained consistent was the individual's perception of parental love, which may have had nothing to do with how loving and caring the parents actually were. It was the belief that the parents were loving which really mattered.

The affections and beliefs of others have and will continue to influence you in pronounced as well as subtle ways. And your beliefs will, likewise, impact on others. In "Meditation 17," John Donne wrote, *"No man is an island, entire of itself; every man is a piece of the continent, a part of the main."* What you do is linked with those from your past and will influence those you meet in the future. I'm going to tell you the story of how just one man touched the lives of thousands of children. A man who was awarded a British knighthood for his generosity. Yet, a man whose acts of altruism may have been fueled by a belief, which might well, have eroded the health of his heart. It is the true story of two people whose beliefs drove their behavior in ways that serve to highlight all the topics discussed in this book. The opening scene is war-torn Europe.

Norman was always the one chosen by his superiors to slip behind enemy lines – not to engage the Germans during WWII, but to seek food for his combat unit. Despite the high risk, he always succeeded, just as he had in civilian life, for he was a perfectionist who couldn't accept failure. Whether it was running his farm in England or enthralling audiences with his trumpet, he excelled. But not when it came to his family. His two young sons were to be deprived of all but his biological contribution to their existence. Like countless others, he succumbed to the allure of an attractive, young woman who lived in the village, a not uncommon scenario which may well have unfolded in your life, as well. What is unique about this particular story, though, is its positive outcome, an outcome that gave meaning and purpose to thousands of children, as well as to the family he abandoned.

Norman not only abandoned his family, but his country. He and his new bride boarded a ship, which took them halfway around the world to a new life in Australia, a life that left behind all traces of his past. Even in the company of his closest friends, he never uttered a word about the wife and sons he left behind. And on the single occasion when his former wife solicited the services of the Red Cross to let him know she had relocated to the United States, he curtly demanded that she never make contact again. As a consequence, he existed as nothing more than an image in the minds of his sons.

And what kind of image? An irresponsible scoundrel? That would certainly be an image their mother would have been more than justified to have fostered. But, no. It was the opposite type of image. The image of a man who could do anything. A brilliant musician. A resourceful soldier. A decorated war hero. A man with a weakness, yet a man of honor. A man who had left, but, perhaps, not before instilling these wonderful traits in his sons. This was their father. Their lineage. And it was shaped entirely by the carefully chosen words of their mother, for their own memories were too fragmented to be of any value.

Why would a woman so wronged be so generous in her praise of a man who was despised by her friends and family? Would this account be a more suitable illustration of denial than beliefs? Perhaps, but I don't think so. You see, Eileen had a rare gift. She was a woman who personified every characteristic of a truly healthy person. She had never known a stranger and saw beauty in those things the average person would overlook. A weathered face sculpted in a cloud. A sparkle in the morning dew. The fragrance of freshly mown grass.

Dead leaves and the shrinking days of October did not signify the inevitable end of yet another of nature's cycles, but the nearness of Christmas. Anyone who knew her would have considered it perfectly normal for Eileen to have seen the good in a man that so many others had demonized. She walked the talk. While acknowledging the faults we all harbor, she believed all people are inherently good – even the ones who hurt her. It wasn't denial. She accepted this unexpected transition in her life in much the same spirit that she endured the nightly bombing of her native London. Instead of dwelling upon doom, she chose to live each day to the hilt, extracting every morsel of pleasure she could from the most unlikely of sources. She could see beyond the rubble around her. And through her beliefs, she enabled others to sometimes share in her gift and remain optimistic and in good humor, even in the midst of despair, for her wartime assignment was organizing games and entertainment in the public bomb shelters.

She did not allow the actions of Norman to become a cancer, to permeate her thoughts and images of the world around her. To take anything away from the hours and days which she viewed as a precious gift from God. And through her stated beliefs and actions, neither would she allow it to shape her children's lives. No, it wasn't denial. It was her acceptance of an image containing the negative, but not denying the positive. She chose to focus her attention on that part most likely to bring pleasure, not despair. By setting this example, she provided her sons with resources to enrich their own lives as well as those of their children. In this way, a belief can be as enduring as a genetic code for the body, a code for the mind. Spirituality is a blueprint, not for creating life, but for interpreting and finding meaning in life.

Norman began a new life in Australia, and with his bride, had two additional sons. He also adopted a young, aboriginal girl who had been abandoned by her family in the rugged Outback. No one, including his closest friends, had any inkling that a single mother struggling to survive with her two young children on the other side of the world was inextricably linked with the handsome musician who disembarked in Western Australia. He had chosen to erase this chapter in his life. I doubt he was successful, though. No amount of time or distance could possibly remove every trace. Surely, young boys and, eventually, men he encountered must have made him pause, wondering if there were a resemblance. A fragrance. A song. Perhaps a color or holiday would occasionally unlock a suppressed memory residing in the inner recesses of his mind.

181

How did he cope? With medications? Or, was he so indifferent that he was able to ignore such images of the past? Highly unlikely for a man possessing the wonderful attributes recalled by Eileen. There is no evidence he turned to pharmacological solutions. Instead, he devoted his life to helping disadvantaged children throughout Australia.

When he first arrived *down under*, he drove delivery trucks for a beer distributor, while continuing to play his trumpet and directing the Western Australia Orchestra. But, he had another calling, which was to help children, especially those who came from broken homes. Upon the conclusion of each workday, he provided them with free music lessons. Those without transportation, he picked up and drove to the local concert hall. At other times, he could be found scavenging for discarded instruments from military and other sources. These then were repaired at his expense and made available to the budding, adolescent musicians. Norman then organized youth orchestras. Not just in Perth, but throughout the entire Australian continent. He was eventually rewarded with the British Empire Medal for his self-sacrifice and efforts on behalf of others.

What possessed him to do all this? To devote his life to helping children? Was it pure altruism or a form of compensation? It's not possible to know with certainty, but, I suspect, it was a combination of both. Eileen always described Norman as being a kind man, but he probably chose children to be the recipients of his generosity, in part, because of his having left his own two young sons.

There was a happy ending for the two of them and for their mother, as well. She remarried an American who brought his instant family home to the United States, where untold opportunities awaited the two boys, opportunities they could never have had in their native England. And Eileen continued to spread goodwill and happiness in every community in which she lived.

Norman and Eileen emerged from the same experience and found satisfaction in helping others. But the similarity ends here. One was fueled, perhaps, by an image of remorse. The other by an image of optimism. Norman's was only a partial solution, a way of moving forward while building a new life. It was not a solution for the probable conflict within him, a conflict that may well have contributed to his eventual heart attack. A close friend thought he brought it upon himself. *"He worked too hard,"* she told me. How ironic that Norman's eventual death was brought about by a damaged heart, while Eileen continued to find meaning in life through an internationally acclaimed entertainment group called *The Young@Heart Chorus.*

Until her death, at the age of 93, Eileen continued to bring joy to others as a member of *The Young@Heart Chorus.* An award-winning documentary released in 2007 is being viewed worldwide, while the remaining cast continues to be in demand throughout Europe and the Pacific Rim, where concert halls from Amsterdam to Sydney fill to capacity whenever the Young@Heart is scheduled. Is the legacy she left behind also one that has been shaped by her beliefs? Undoubtedly. This is hardly the behavior of a person who would have chosen to wallow in self-pity. Nor of a person who would have wasted untold energy seeking retribution. No. The beliefs that enabled her to emerge unscathed from WWII and the restructuring of her own life continued to enable her to spread joy and happiness to others.

What type of life do you want to lead? Eileen's or Norman's? Are your beliefs going to stimulate physical and spiritual growth, or in subtle ways erode your health? In what ways have your beliefs been shaped by those who have touched your life? And how healthy were those people? Was it a Norman or an Eileen? In my life, it has been my mother - Eileen.

No matter what your belief, ultimately, it should enable you to lead a healthier, more productive, and enriched life and to achieve goals consistent with your values. Start by asking yourself, *"What do I want out of life?"* Many people live their entire lives without ever asking this essential question. As a result, their lives become a series of events dictated by external circumstances, instead of inner needs and desires. Unless you know what your inner desires are, you have no choice but to bounce from one activity to another. You are forced to accept whatever comes your way. That may not always be bad, but why not stack the odds in favor of what you define as success? Identify your personal goals. Make them realistic and assign a time frame.

In my lifetime, I want to _____.

Prior to retirement, I want to _____.

Before my children have left home, I want to _____.

By _____ *I want to* _____.

And once again, ask yourself these questions:

- Are these goals attainable?
- Are these my goals or those of someone else?
- Are they stated concisely and as a positive objective?
- Am I willing to begin now? If not, under what circumstances will I begin?
- Am I willing to make changes in my life to achieve my goals?
- Are my goals consistent with my beliefs and values?
- Do any of my goals conflict with each other?

- What am I willing to give up to achieve my goal?

Continue to assess your goals on a regular basis – not because I'm advising you to but because you recognize the need to and because you want to. Life is not a dress rehearsal. Live each moment as though it is your last, but assume it will go on forever. And make sure those moments are consistent with your beliefs. Earlier, I suggested you complete some incomplete statements that I provided to assist in identifying your beliefs. Now, I'll tell you how I would complete them.

People are inherently good, but not without imperfections. Judge a person based upon his total contribution, not on the basis of one or two attributes. And be forgiving. We all make mistakes.

Stress is a natural part of life. It is a stimulus for growth. But make certain you allow time to recover. That's when the stress-stimulated growth actually occurs.

Relationships are always changing. You married a friend and lover, who later became a parent. We change constantly and need to prepare for times when the relationship may be more or less than what it was at another phase.

The world would be a better place to live if people adopted a very simple philosophy espoused by Rotary International, an organization committed to serving others. It's called the 4-way test, and it is a good starting point as you consider the decisions you make, what you will say, and what you will do.

- Is it the truth?
- Is it fair to all concerned?
- Will it build goodwill and better friendships?
- Will it be beneficial to all concerned?

And in completing the final statement, *I am* a husband and father. A son and brother. A scientist and friend. Include all the roles you play in life as you ask that important question, *"Who am I?"*

As you follow my recommendations for assessing your beliefs and setting goals, your ultimate objective should be never to have to write the kind of letter written by Erma Bombeck before losing her battle with cancer:

IF I HAD MY LIFE TO LIVE OVER
by Erma Bombeck

I would have talked less and listened more.
I would have invited friends over to dinner even if the carpet was stained and the sofa faded.
I would have eaten the popcorn in the 'good' living room and worried much less about the dirt when someone wanted to light a fire in the fireplace.
I would have taken the time to listen to my grandfather ramble about his youth.
I would never have insisted the car windows be rolled up on a summer day because my hair had just been teased and sprayed.
I would have burned the pink candle sculpted like a rose before it melted in storage.
I would have sat on the lawn with my children and not worried about grass stains.
I would have cried and laughed less while watching television – and more while watching life.
I would have shared more of the responsibility carried by my husband.
I would have gone to bed when I was sick instead of pretending the earth would go into a holding pattern if I weren't there for the day.
I would never have bought anything just because it was practical, wouldn't show soil, or was guaranteed to last a lifetime.
Instead of wishing away nine months of pregnancy, I'd have cherished every moment and realized that the wonderment growing inside me was the only chance in life to assist God in a miracle.
When my kids kissed me impetuously, I would never have said, "Later. Now go get washed up for dinner."
There would have been more "I love you's"... more "I'm sorry's"...but mostly, given another shot at life, I would seize every minute...look at it and really see it...live it...and never give it back.

Printed in the United States
139423LV00001B/2/P

9 781424 304646